Pausing...

Long Enough

to Notice

TERESA D. HUGGINS

Published by
Success Talks Publishing
Cleveland, Ohio

Cover and Book Design by Autumn Lew, Graphic Minion Studios.
Autumn@GraphicMinion.com

Printed in the United States of America

First Edition

Library of Congress Cataloguing-in-Publication Data

Huggins, Teresa D.
      Pausing…Long Enough to Notice
  Teresa D. Huggins. – 1ˢᵗ ed.
          p. cm. – (Success Talks Publishing; v. 1)
      LCCN: 2008930103
      ISBN: 978-0-9673198-4-1

  1. Inspiration.   2. Self-Help.

Acknowledgements

It is with gratitude that I prepare this book for the world; gratitude for all who have influenced my life. The stories within this book came from simple conversations, moments shared with loved ones, and from a dream stirring in my soul.

I share gratitude for God who whispered this dream into my awareness, who shared that life is about living in the moment, embracing the experiences that we have each day, capturing the spirit of life and love and sharing them for others to enjoy.

I share gratitude for Bill, my husband, who took care of so many details while I was writing and writing. His gift of unconditional love inspires the flow of the writings within this book. His commitment to creating a joy-filled home fills my heart with love. His support of my vision transformed this book from an idea to reality!

I share gratitude for Tara and Mike, my children, who bring joy and laughter into my life, who teach me to notice the magical moments of a day. Their visions and their spirits open my creative channels to see beyond what others may see, to feel the sparkle in an experience, and to hear the message within the words. To your future, I offer you all you can imagine. You are loved for being you!

I share gratitude for my family and friends, near and far, and too many to mention each one individually. Your presence in my life is a gift that inspired me to write! The stories within were influenced by our conversations, our walks, our travels and our shared journeys. You have given me confidence to know that people will receive what they seek when they read the stories within the covers. For my manifestation group: Your unwavering support and encouragement through the uncertain moments, your creative strategies, and your transformative ideas brought me to a place where I trust the essence of this book.

I share gratitude for my Leaders for Life family. The essence of who you are and the spirit you bring to this planet fill my heart with love. Your commitment to creating a brighter future for our world inspires me; your dedicated support of one another touch my soul. For the college students and adults who supported the vision of L4L, I hold a special place in my heart for you. You are within the stories of this book. As I paused and remembered our shared experiences, your love is captured within the journey of these writings.

I share gratitude for Jack Canfield for being a teacher with a capital T, for sharing your creative ideas and support over the years, for inspiring me to live my dreams! Your simple statements of encouragement resonated within me as I created this book. To all my friends that I met at the Canfield Trainings, your support from afar is felt deep within my spirit. Your courage to pursue your dreams inspired me to do the same.

I share gratitude for Sandra Zimlich of Success Talks, Inc. and Autumn Lew of Graphic Minion Studios. Your creative genius captured the spirit of this book. Your diligence to detail has resulted in a product that will open hearts and minds. Your patience as we nurtured this book is appreciated.

I share gratitude for the people who pass me on my journey of life, who share time and space with me even though I don't know your name. You are included in the stories. As I noticed you, I felt your joy, heard your laughter, sensed your fear and wondered about your dreams. To those who have gone before me, your spirits are within the messages of this book. Your lessons resonate within my being and your essence is felt in the sunlight as it reflects on the ripples in the water. The lessons remain beyond the moments we shared.

I share gratitude for all who will read this book and open their hearts to the possibilities within a moment. May you live life fully, remembering to "pause" and notice the world you are creating every day.

Table of Contents

Introduction: 1

Section One: Noticing the Sparkling Moments

Faces 5

Hurrying Through Life 6

Good Morning Spring 8

Easter Sunrise Morning 10

A New Dawning 14

Peeking Through the Window: A Full Moon Experience 16

Early Morning Awakening 19

April Morn 21

There is Always a Way 23

Morning in the Mountains 26

Section Two: Releasing the Challenges

Time to Create 31

A New Vision 33

Let it Snow 35

After the Storm 38

Forgiveness 40

The Swirl of Turbulence 41

Oversized Load 42

Section Three: Transforming Obstacles into Opportunities

Act Now 46

After the Attack: September 11, 2001 48

Angel's Landing 50

Looking Beyond 55

Beyond the Fog 59

Sparkles After the Storm 61

The Midst of the Mountains 63

Through the Rain 65

With the Spirit of Childhood 67

Section Four: *Exploring New Dreams, New Pathways to Self*

Renewal Moments 71

The Dance of a Butterfly 73

The Dream, Dare, and Dance Journey 75

Remembering the Light 76

Parallel Paths 81

Pathways 84

Why Do They Tell Me? 85

Section Five: *Appreciating Angelic Moments*

A Gift from the Ocean 88

I Am the Wind: Dedicated to Loved Ones Who Left Before Us 90

Millie's Music 92

Serenity 94

The Gift of Song 96

The Light of Love 98

The Sparkling Moments 101

Opening and Releasing 102

Section Six: *Creating the Ripple Effect*

Living Passionately 109

Living with Heart 111

Minnowbrook Memories 114

One by One 116

Genuine Love 118

Messages Within the Chaos 120

Soul Connections 123

The Light of a New Day 124

The Ripple Effect 126

The Stream of Allowing 128

Unconditional Love of Friends 130

Until the Next Rainbow 131

Within the Pause 133

Introduction

As we vacationed in Virginia, I was drawn to the purple trees that lined the highway. After a long blustery winter in New York, we left the mud-covered brown grass and barren trees for warmer temperatures. I was mesmerized by the brilliance of the purple blossoms on the tree. "Bill, pull over. I want to take a photo of the majestic trees." With the camera on my cell phone, I took photos and looked forward to seeing if we could grow these same magnificent trees on our property in New York. When we returned home, I showed the photo to a friend who was a horticulturist and asked, "What are these trees? Can we plant them here?" The puzzled look on his face and his next question, "You are kidding me, right?" confused me. "Yes, I really want to see these trees blossom on my property in the spring." He began to laugh and said, "Teresa, they are all over town! They will blossom here in about two weeks!" I was shocked. I had never noticed them! Upon reflection, I realized that they blossomed in May, a busy time for me at work and with local service projects that I supported. Every day I drove to work passing the beautiful blossoms and never noticed. Instead, I was rehearsing the day, focusing on what was next, going over my children's schedule or thinking about something else. I was so engrossed in "doing" that I allowed the beauty around me to fade into the horizon. I never saw it, never experienced its beauty nor ever allowed myself time enough to just "be"!

After "graduating" from a twenty-one year career in public education, I began the pursuit of my dream to create the visions stored within my heart. That's when I began to notice. I began to slow down and invited life to unfold. Still accomplishing much, yet living with greater awareness of a balanced life, I discovered the power of living from a state of "being." I noticed more in life and experienced the hidden messages within ordinary experiences. Allowing myself to enjoy life, trust the process, and follow my intuition, I embraced the power of breathing in the beauty that surrounded me and felt the feelings that emerged from a simple moment.

While in the process of writing another book, this book began to take form. By pausing for a moment each day and paying attention to the seemingly ordinary experiences, gentle nudges of intuition emerged. Stories unfolded effortlessly. Believing the stories flowed from the divine, sometimes they emerged so quickly that my fingers danced across the keyboard and the essence was captured in a few minutes. It is my intention that you will receive answers you seek when you read the stories enclosed within the covers of this book. It is my hope that you will take a moment each day to notice the dance of a butterfly, the whisper of the wind as it kisses the grass, and the glimmer of sunlight on a lake. It is my desire that you will invite nature to speak to you, to offer you comfort on a challenging day or to give you the gift that in a moment, life can be transformed.

As you open the pages of this book, you may want to ask a question and discover the answer within. You may want to read a story and allow its message to resonate within your heart. The journey is yours. My wish for you is to breathe in the beauty of this day. Listen to the whispers of your heart and embrace the possibility of your dreams becoming your reality…when you pause…long enough to notice!

Noticing
the Sparkling Moments

⤙ Faces

In the serenity of this night, the essence of life's experiences weave through my mind, my heart and my soul.

Faces...faces of individuals yearning to be free of limits that hold them back from fully living, from freely experiencing the dance of joy.

Faces...faces of individuals who yearn to catapult their dreams as they expand their business, transform their relationships, and discover the passion within their hearts.

Faces...faces of young people who dream BIG and who feel the excitement of creating a future filled with possibilities, leaders living from their hearts, companies that care about the world, and families that speak with compassion for one another.

Faces...faces of friends who support and genuinely care, who listen without judgment, who serve without thought of return, who encourage when the answers seem far away.

Faces...faces of loved ones who let us ramble when we are confused, who know when to share a hug, and listen without comment, who take care of the little things so the bigger dreams can be created.

✎ Hurrying Through Life

We journey through life hurrying on to the next task, the next appointment, the next item on our "to do" list. In our actions of "doing" we miss "being." We feel like we are achieving many victories checking off our accomplishments. Searching for that sense of calm and relaxation that we seek when we accomplish our goals, we wonder when we will feel a genuine sense of serenity. Inner contentment is our wish. We dream of the days gone by when we breathed deeply and cherished fondly. In our busyness (business) of life, we forgot to notice the moon in the sky in the early morning. We forgot to watch the wisps of snow dance across the land, gently carried by the wind with its majestic tones as the wind connects with the earth. We forgot to ponder the meaning of a "dead" tree that is a resting stop for birds in flight. We forgot to turn around and notice the rising sun peering through the dormant maple trees brushing them with colors of gold, orange, and red, just like they had a few months ago. In our desire to feel accomplished, we forgot to realize the miracle of life, of friends, and of nature.

As we focus on our list of "to do's," we forget to "be." It is in our *beingness* that we are real. It is in our *beingness* that we let go of the need to complete #22 on our list. I wonder if we took a few moments "to be," if we would achieve more, rest assured each night that as the next day unfolds, more sparkling moments will appear in our path, the flickering light of a tower in a distance, the reflection of the sun turning a dark morning into a hue of color.

Just as the seasons change the landscape of our outer world, the essence of living, changes our inner structure. As the world rests in the northern winter, we know that spring will blossom once again. Grass will sprout, butterflies will dance, and life will be renewed. The darkness of night reminds us to rest and the rays of sunshine remind us to embrace the new opportunities of the day. The possibilities of miracles are on the horizon with each tree that sprouts a life, with each bulb that blooms a flower, and with each person that hopes for a new outcome, a new healthy life.

May your today be filled with moments of *beingness*, moments of ah-hah sensations, moments of letting go and letting God. May today be filled with reminders of what is to come, of what is possible, of what lies ahead. May today be filled with an inner awareness of light and love that connects one human to another. May today be filled with friendship that reminds others we are never alone when the connections of the heart remain.

✎ Good Morning Spring

In the quiet of the morning, the full moon peers through the window as the day begins to unfold. Stars still twinkle high in the sky as the quiet of the night creates a blanket of silence on planet earth. In an hour, the sun will dawn, the morning will open, lives will awake and choices will be made. With each day, we have an opportunity to begin anew as we await the blossoming of our experiences.

Today, spring begins in Clinton, New York. The warmth of the sun lifts the spirits of many who were hoping for a breath of fresh air, a relief from the cold snaps of morning. The birds sing songs of joy as they communicate to one another; they share joy with those who slow down long enough to listen. One bird seems to say "hello" while another responds "I am here." A simple interaction offers reassurance and a connection of spirit that reminds us how simply we can transform a moment in time. Connecting with another who brightens our day is a simple act that can alter a challenging moment.

Yes, awaking to the warm sun, the gentle breeze jostles the shrubs that have survived the harsh zip of winter. The brown grass that was hidden under snow bathes in the rays of the sun and begins to emerge as a deeper green stretching toward the sun, reminding us that the cycle of recovery exists within each of us. The barren trees reach upward and stretch toward the light as their hidden buds begin to emerge from within their branches. Patiently, the trees that were once filled with leaves recreate themselves.

The journey of nature in spring reminds us of the simplicity of the life cycle. Regardless of what has been, they focus on their journey of new birth, resilient spirit and connection to the oneness of the universe. Imagine if we remained true within our own missions during the dark times, the days when obstacles just seem to present themselves. Imagine if we held the image of a maple tree in upstate New York in our vision. It all begins with a barren tree in spring focused on blossoming into the beauty that renews one's spirit to see the healing green leaves reappear. In summer, this same tree provides shade for people enjoying a day at the park, and then blossoms into a rainbow of colors in the days of autumn as the cold night kiss the green leaves and magically reappear as the colors of harvest, red, yellow, gold and burgundy. As the leaves dance in the sky and fall from the trees, the crunch of dried leaves remind us that the brisk days of winter are soon upon us. And, the cycle begins again.

Yes, the warm gentle breeze of this spring day reminds me of the power to renew our spirits, revisit our dreams and transform our thoughts into the realm of possibility. As a fuzzy bumble bee whizzes by, I am reminded that they anatomically are "unable" to fly and choose to do so anyway. As the robins gather on my lawn, I wonder if they rediscovered their path here and if they were the ones that created the brilliant blue eggs in our shrubs last spring. As the butterfly dances in the wind, I wonder what adventure it might have experienced to get here.

To live with the confidence of the smallest of nature's creatures, to notice the buds on a tree and remember our inner strength, to pause and listen to the whisper of the wind and to dance to the music of the symphony of birds perching on a tree branch. This is to be truly living in the present moment on this glorious day of spring, trusting that all will beautifully unfold in this journey we call life.

⊹ Easter Sunrise Morning

As the star-speckled sky dances high above me, life remains still in the darkness. Life rests all around as the full moon's rays bring hope to our planet earth. In silence, the earth rests, people renew in their sleep and life pauses for a moment before they begin their day. As I drive in the darkness guiding the car along the curves of this mountain road, the branches of the tree form a silhouette against the opaque mountains. A fawn on the side of the road peeks her head up and notices the head-lights, as she calmly provides herself with nourishment for her own existence. She is unencumbered by the world around her, in simple form, reminding us of the power of one's focus and intention of behavior, fully aware of her surroundings and yet unobtrusive to others. Unconcerned about the individuals resting in the homes to her right and to her left, she is simply being who she is meant to be.

As I climb the mountain road, passing homes nestled in the sides of the hill, realizing someone designed this beautiful landscaped paradise, respecting the needs of nature, and joining human with earth, I am empowered to dream bigger, to create the vision that is stored within my heart. On this Easter morn, the full moon hides behind the passing clouds that seem to swim in the sky as the gentle wind allows one to capture a snapshot of the moon as the wispy clouds float by.

On this dark morning, the air resonates with hope for a future of peace and love, hope for wellness for all who are sick, and hope for the creation of dreams yet to unfold. On this dark morning, the mountains embrace the individuals who are resting within its valley. The earth provides the foundation for the trees that are stretching toward heaven yearning to bud forth and blossom, like the trees covered with glorious purple buds that I have noticed down below.

People gather on the mountain top joining small town Elkton, Virginians with visitors from the homes below. All welcome, no judgments, no expectations, friends hugging friends as they greet on this early morn. Greetings all around for those we yet to meet. No strangers here, only new people on the path of life. People joining together for the possibility of being a witness to the truths of life, a powerful message for me as I move forward with my writing and my messages for others to be uninhibited in life and open to the possibilities.

As the morning opens, the lights from the homes delicately placed on the mountain side sparkle, the mist rises from the valley in the distance as if removing the layers of doubt and uncertainty from the day before to greet a new morning. With each evening of rest, we can release all the concerns; open ourselves to new beginnings of a spectacular day. As we inhale the beauty that surrounds us, we are filled with the possibility of creating a day just as we desire.

People worship, sing under the stars. Some climb the trail for a greater view. Some stay in the parking lot and share conversation about loved ones and even debate who bakes the best hot cross buns. The sun gloriously blossoms behind the mountain; the sky opens to a blue hue in just a moment's time. The sun softens the clouds above painting the surfaces in a pink hue. As God paints the sky with a multitude of color, we are reminded of the power of faith and trust in all that can be.

As we stand at our vantage point on planet earth, the sun widens its rays and causes this writer to squint and see bubbles on this page. Fully embraced in the light of a new day, a new vision emerges, a realization that with every beautiful moment we experience in life, we have the power to share that with another, to offer thanks for the moments of a day and to reach out even when we are uncertain. Laughter fills the air; joy is shared between friends, connections of the heart offer the light of the sunrise to radiate from within to be shared with all. A local approaches a tourist and within a minute they find a conversation of shared travels in common. One by one, people connect sharing stories of hospital experiences, recipe swapping, or just being fully present in the glorious sunrise that blossoms in the sky.

In 30 minutes the earth will be awake, transforming from a darkened sky silhouetted by the rolling mountains to the opening of a warm Easter day about to unfold. Families will share special meals; children will search for Easter eggs and baskets that were delivered by the bunny. There will be little ones in their frilly clothes that grandmas and grandpas ooh and ah over, while the kids itch in the lace of the new clothes, yearning for the time when "play clothes" can be worn after dinner. A memory of my very own Grandma Graham enters my mind...

The slumber of winter rests and the resilience of spring awakens as the birds sing in the distance, calling one another to join in the chorus of the early morning. The gracious people have left, yet their spirit remains. Where there was once a joining of souls for the common purpose of worship, there is the reflection of the sun on the pavement. The shadows of the trees kiss the pavement below and the sun glistens on the tiniest blades of grass. Yes, they are no longer here, yet their essence remains - support for others, conviction to their faith, awe for the magical moments of nature and a sense of humor that created a vibration of joy within my heart.

Isn't that so in life? We can journey on a new path, uncertain where it is going to lead, trusting our intuition that it is the one we are meant to be on, and while we journey, we receive gifts that we yearn for. Individuals without names, yet full of spirit reminded me of the gifts of friendship and family, the power of a simple interaction and the magnificence of nature. Their simple presence is a witness to the power of God's love and the gratefulness that emanated from them reminded me how one's actions speak very loud to those who surround us. While I never met any of the people, I was touched by their light. When we open ourselves to connect fully and with an acceptance for all who cross our path, we notice the sincerity of a hug shared among neighbors, hear the scamper of a squirrel that just startled me and feel the gratitude for the memories that resonate within my being as I view the gentle horizon of the mountains.

✎ A New Dawning

We experience life with a desire to accomplish goals, achieve more, see more, and be more. Sometimes, we become so absorbed with the tasks at hand, that a day just disappears… *Poof*, it is gone and we wonder how all that unfolded in one day was possible. Sometimes our days are filled with challenges, "improvement opportunities" and when we rest at night, our minds swirl with the "what ifs" and "could I only have," perhaps creating a struggle to find a comfortable night of rest. Sometimes we rethink our choices, reconsider our actions, and contemplate all that has unfolded. We live in the past, wondering, wishing if it could have been different, unsettled with unspoken messages swirling in our mind. We replay conversations in our mind, interactions with others, situations that "showed up," and we wonder how we could have changed it, altered it, refocused it, and reconstructed it. In these times that we live in the past, we miss the opportunities of the new day.

Sometimes we allow experiences that are out of our control to burden us like heavy darkened clouds that envelope majestic mountains. Each morning is an opportunity to remember a bright skyline with varying shades of blue glaze atop a mountain. The puffy clouds float gently by instead of the stagnant storm clouds with their threatening presence. In a moment, of "getting out of our own way" we can notice. We notice that the unsettled feeling of yesterday doesn't need to stay within us. The burdens of days gone by no longer need to find home within our being. The misconstrued slightly altered conversations of miscommunication no longer need to embrace our imagination.

A blossoming new morning leads way for a new focus to appear, a new dawning of possible solutions, a new presence of hope and determination. Sometimes we wander through life in our heads, making up stories, redesigning the storyline to fit our current mode of desire. Sometimes we contemplate a certain situation, an interaction, or life event so many times that the essence of what really took place is lost in the conversion of our mind wanting to make sense of it all.

All it takes is an inner commitment to begin each day with a renewed sense of hope, a recommitment to living life as a "solution creator," an intrinsic commitment to notice the delicate moments of a day. As I awake and glimpse at the horizon, I breathe in the crisp new air. I quiet my mind and realize a chorus of birds is opening the day. I breathe deeply and exhale any left over concerns in my mind. I open my heart to the magic of this moment, fully understanding that this one particular moment will never be repeated, never be embraced and I am the one that has a choice.

I can inhale the beauty of this new moment with joy, peace and love in my heart or I can remain within the confines of my mind as it stays logged into a previous moment. I choose to inhale the crisp air, notice the dew on the rock, and the angle of the little purple flower that endures regardless of the temperature or directness of the sun. It peeks around the shade of the transforming maple tree and finds its own light, grows into the light. It discovers a solution so that it may provide beauty for a passerby who happens to notice.

I can inhale the beauty of this morning and notice in the distance that the sun rays peeking through a cloud leave a rainbow on the dew-laden grass. I can inhale the crispness of this morning and offer gratitude for the changing of the seasons that many in the world have never experienced. I can inhale the calm around me, the serenity of a moment in nature.

Yes, in the new dawning of this day, I can surrender to the journey, staying present in the moment, capturing the possibility of an answer unfolding during this day. Believing that each day is truly a gift to experience, fully and openly, I embrace all that lies ahead.

ᴥ Peeking Through the Window: A Full Moon Experience

The night sky illuminates with the vibrancy of the full moon stretching its light to every corner of the planet. The iridescent light of the moon peeks through the window radiating its beams into our home. As I peek into the moonlit night, I can see the shine of the light sending a glow in four directions appearing as a cross, a spiritual symbol for many. In each direction, its light pulsates, offering a glow to the sky and earth. Its aura radiates in every direction giving the illusion of light emanating from its being.

Transfixed by the beauty of the moon's light, breathing in the source, I inhale the essence of this calming experience. Noticing the reflection on the earth below, the evergreens stand firmly and the light shines between the blades of grass, creating a pattern in the field.

As we gently fall to sleep, the moon caresses our bodies with the reminder that while we rest, nature continues to dance through the night. Brilliant light above and shadows below create illusions on our land. The moon radiates in every direction forming a cross in the sky. Faith fills the sky. Its rays are far reaching beyond this moment in time. Its balanced circle of brilliant white light stretches…reaching, growing in every direction. Silent, suspended in air, magical…wherever one looks, in their own corner of the world, the light can be felt. Its rays send healing vibrations to every corner of this planet. In the silence of this night, people rest, bathed in the aura of the moon. I look upward again into the sky and the cross has transformed into a heavenly glow, resembling the rays of the sun, yet only in hues of white. My eyes are drawn into the core of the moon, and for a moment, the features on the moon's surface seem to become one with Earth.

Just as quickly as the moon peeked through my window, it hides behind a passing cloud, creating an illusion that it is faintly there, yet knowing it is fully present. Sometimes in life we allow our light to dim as our minds swirl with doubt and confusion. Sometimes in life we forget that our light can radiate and brighten an otherwise dreary day.

As I connect with the rays of the moon, during this 3:33 AM moment, life pauses, the earth seems to stand still. Crickets sing to one another, stars vibrate in the sky; the moon's rays create silhouettes on the earth. In this moment, the sky connects with earth, no longer separate; the light of the moon stretches and bathes the earth with a resilient spirit.

Sparkling rays of peace fall to the earth.

As people sleep, dreams dance and solutions flow.

A vibration of healing radiates for all to breathe in.

Light fills the crevices within a body that asks for healing.

Light washes away the uncertainty that plagues a mind.

Light fills the emptiness of an empty heart.

Light opens for connection with the divine.

Light replaces darkness in the soul.

Light reminds us that dreams stretch beyond this moment in time.

One day, long ago, someone believed "we can travel to the moon" and by persevering, by transcending the doubt of others, by surpassing the insurmountable challenges...one day, long ago, man stepped on the moon....its light fills the earth below. What else is possible when you believe?

As we pause and notice, the moon seems to draw closer, connected to the inner brilliance that we all share with this earth, the brilliance that transcends a moment in time, a location, a person, an event. Yes, as the light of the moon stretches to every corner of this planet, so does our light. One simple action, one kind conversation, one dream shared with another...stretching, reaching, believing.

The moon appears to be only in my backyard, yet reality captures my attention again and reminds me that millions of people throughout the planet may look at the moon and receive its healing vibrations. This moment in time transcends space as we know it. A realization that what may appear as separate is actually connected…a connected universe, one where an experience shared by one can be felt by many. A connected universe passing in time creates a ripple for all to feel, an essence of light for all to experience.

↭ Early Morning Awakening

As I bike this early morning, the sun lifts over the mountains. As the sun's rays lift upward, they seem to creep from behind the mountain. I recall the warmth of the sunset from last night and feel the brisk temperature of this crisp morning, welcoming the warmth of the day that is awakening. As the clouds separate, a brilliant blue sky is revealed. As moisture evaporates and the dew of a chilly September night lifts, a resilient valley is revealed. The silhouette of the mountains surround this tiny town of Stowe, Vermont and although the green trees appear darkened, I trust that in a few weeks the landscape will resemble lollipops of red, orange, yellow, and burgundy as the trees blossom with their autumn foliage. Evergreens reach upward as if connecting heaven with earth. A single leaf shaped like a heart rests on the bike path, reminding me to live with heart no matter where I journey. The tiniest purple and yellow blossoms discover their inner strength and stretch opening to a new day.

As I pause on the trail and notice the creek beside me, I observe the water flowing effortlessly. Meandering, it finds its way as it travels around and over the rocks, not allowing them to be obstacles in its path. The droplets of water carry one another joining together, merging to create a new union as they travel to a shared destiny downstream. Within the stillness of this early morning, the babbling brook brings comfort to this new day. As the water caresses the shoreline, a leaf is carried in its path. The water trickles between the rocks, creating mini-waterfalls as the elevation of the creek changes. Gracefully blending in harmony, coming from different sources, yet joining as one, the journey unfolds. Trusting its path, the placid water slides down the rocks, dancing over the larger rocks creating a fountain of sparkles, a cascade of possibilities. It's as if joyful laughter could vibrate from this dance. A moth skims the water and skates across its surface, yearning to be free, yet finds itself creating ripples of water that vibrate beyond its tiny being. Its legs paddle with all its strength, determined to be in control of its path, knowing that it could easily be carried away.

I find myself imagining; pondering the miracle of it all. If a little moth can create a vibration within the water, if a tiny flower can grow through a concrete surface, and if a bee flying nearby can alter our path, imagine what we can achieve. If we remember that each new morning is an opportunity to begin again, to discover solutions we seek, to reconnect with one another, to forgive and love again. Imagine if we pause long enough to notice the simplicity of nature. I breathe in the light of this new day. I pause long enough to notice a butterfly in flight dancing from flower to flower. I commit to creating time to have a heartfelt conversation with a loved one, and promise to notice the sparkle within their eyes.

↞ April Morn

The morning is crisp with a hint of spring in the air. As I lace my new running shoes, I notice three robins returning from their winter travels. I inhale the fresh air and begin a new journey. Down the road I travel with a quicker pace and a new belief. I notice a blue jay in the tree and hear the whisper of the wind. My surroundings take on a new appearance at 5:45 AM, noticing so many details are missed as I'm flying through my normal routine of a day. Inhaling deeply, listening to the quiet and calm, wondering what lies ahead, I continue my pace captured in a sparkling moment of awareness. The sun peeks from beneath the clouds capturing radiance across the sky that reminds me of the power hidden within and beyond.

The sky is filled with a rainbow of yellow, red, and orange. The light shines brightly and clouds float away. What a way to begin the first day of April. I felt renewed and ready to accept the opportunities ahead. Sometimes a day can begin so quietly, so peacefully, even though we might feel that we are being bombarded by challenges. I take a moment to recapture the presence of the calming morn, knowing that the clouds that appear gray, will later in the day disappear. As I look out my window and watch the sky darken, I wonder what happened to the glorious sunrise. Where are the chirping birds and the calm of the early morn? The rain begins and I find myself pondering life.

I wonder how often I forget about the "sunrises" of life, those delightful moments, those refreshing *ah-hah* moments. I look at the rain, yet recall the power of beautiful nature which I experienced only a few hours earlier. I see the storm ahead, yet feel the peace within my heart, remembering the robins, symbolic of the cycle of this earth. In the moment that

I see the rain, I pause and celebrate the new beginnings of this spring-time, committing to pause for a moment each day and renew with the power of the birth of spring.

As we walk through life, or sometimes "run" through life from task to task, let us discover and appreciate the new beginning of a day, notice the chirping of a bird or the laughter of children. Take a moment to rekindle the feel of a hug, the smile of a friend, or the rebirth of a dream. When we experience the "storms" of life, we can picture the power of a new day and begin the internal power of rebirth, of healing. When we experience the "race" of life, pause long enough to notice the wind kissing the grass, the blossom of spring flowers, or the warmth of the sun on your face. When we are searching for answers, be open to the messages which nature may present to you. May the sparkle of the sun on a fresh spring day renew your spirit.

✧ There is Always a Way

As I climbed the rocky path, I considered the power of nature. So often, we get tied up in the challenges of life and forget that there are solutions around every corner. I noticed tiny blades of grass popping through the soil, evidence that when there is will, there is a way. I picked up a tiny acorn that held the potential to one day become a strong oak tree. I wondered how often we remember that the youth we work with are just like the tiny acorns in the forest, an open seed waiting to be planted and nurtured with wisdom, knowledge, and love.

As I climbed higher, there were more brown rocks and less green vegetation. I noticed a tree growing through a rock. A good reminder that just because you cannot see something, does not mean it isn't there. As I examined the roots of the tree, I noticed it resembled a hand grasping for support. The tree emerged between the cracks of the rock and meandered around searching for soil to firmly call home. In life, we often become strongest when there is another to support us along the way. I kneeled to examine this phenomenon so clearly apparent in nature. I was startled by a gray grasshopper, speckled to blend in with rocks. As it jumped, making a sound, it opened its wings like a yellow and green butterfly. Its strength was noticeable as it hopped from rock to rock, seemingly unaware of my presence. I was mesmerized by the confidence that this insect seemed to possess as it found its own path in the woods. When we believe that we can forge ahead even though the path may be rocky, we discover that the power within us is stronger than we might ever imagine.

I continued my hike and discovered there was actually another path. Less rigorous. I was unfamiliar with this territory; I didn't know there was another way. I resolved to adjust to the terrain that lay ahead. Just as when we dream in life, we often forge ahead without really knowing the best path, the proper direction, we just continue believing, knowing that we will one day reach our destination.

I discovered that I had actually been on the less traveled path, the more rigorous journey, yet I still reached the top and fulfilled my goal. As I caught my breath and inhaled the majestic view of the mountains and lake, discovering that what I thought was the final destination was actually a resting spot. I realized that with a few more steps, I had a panoramic view at the summit. Sometimes in life what we think is the best experience may only be the beginning of further discovery, of understanding that life is filled with many possibilities, many paths and many solutions.

As I merged onto a new trail, I crossed over the top of the mountain and discovered a spectacular view of the lake. If I had stopped at my original location, I wouldn't have met the individuals who shared that there was another way to reach the top. I explored the remnants of an old stone house, built in 1926 for shelter for hikers. I found myself wondering how they would have brought the products up the trail. How did they endure the strong winds? The roof blew off yet the remaining walls still offer protection from a chilly windy day. They were able to defy the odds. It was a gentle reminder of staying committed to a dream.

People choose different paths and can still reach similar goals. Following the path that seems to fit our desires can create the lessons that are meant to unfold. It was my journey on that crisp autumn day to notice the tree poking through the rock, the acorn, and the stretch of rock that invited me to discover my own inner strength. It was my time to rediscover the power of individual commitment and persistence to get to the top.

When I finally came down the path, the path I never noticed on my accent, I exited out of the forest - right next to my car! I went left yet never looked right. How often in life is a solution possible yet we never discovered or considered it? How often in life do we keep our eyes on one path when another may be right before us or close by? How often is there a fork in our path? Sometimes there is an obstacle in our path, like a dead tree that we climb over, and we realize that by making another choice, we find a way to reach our destination. Ah, yes. There is always a way to a dream!

✧ Morning in the Mountains

I awaken. There is crispness in the air as the sun sparkles on the majestic mountain offering depth and stature to the evergreen trees that point to heaven. Colorful birds welcome the day in unison creating a chorus of song that can only be achieved by a blending of talents, a connection of spirits, seemingly orchestrated in harmony, yet independent on their own. They sing of peace and hope, resilience and strength.

A lone pine tree stands above the rest, reaching beyond the blend of the forest. As light grows into day, liveliness appears, warmth covers the mountain. In a distance, the repetitive roll of wheels along a highway can be heard interrupting the serenity of the new day. The parking lot is filled with vehicles of people on journeys, exploring new territories, enjoying the adventures along the way.

With the gentle mist of the cold evening now behind us, steam rises from the roof, radiating and dissipating into the early morning air. A single gazebo stands quiet with memories of weddings on days gone by swirling in its mist. A reflective spot lays dormant waiting for the next guests to appear.

As I rediscover the wonder of a new day, I consider the rhythm of life, the opening that occurs each morning. Nature rests at night, renewing its energy and opening to the greatness of a new day. For a moment, I sit in silence on a balcony, listening to the sounds of nature rekindling the fresh spirit that dances within me. Reminded that life changes with every moment, nature speaks gently to the awareness that we experience cycles of living, seasons of life, and moments where the memories of a day gone by merge into the unfurling of a new day. Reminded to remain open to the messages of the song of a bird, the lifting of fog, or the sun's reflection peeking through the trees, I decide that this is what it's like to be fully present in the moment of the dawning of a new day.

Releasing
the Challenges

↬ Time to Create

The wind jostling through the trees on this late summer evening whispers like the sounds of the waves kissing a shoreline. In a moment, I am transported to the beach of California even though I am resting in New York. In one week's time, I have embarked on a transformational journey that carried me to the beaches of the California shoreline and to the beaches of Lake Ontario in northern New York. No longer am I contained to my little corner of the world. I am connected shore to shore, experience to experience, human to human, soul to soul. A connection transcends the journey and remains in one's heart. A conversation swirls within our mind long after the experience is shared. A calming, supportive smile that radiates "I am here for you," resonates with each stranger we meet.

As I rest on this evening with my window open. I feel the crisp breeze as it gently covers my entire being. With each swirl of wind, it seems to whisk away any concerns of what was or what will be. It sprinkles hope in my soul and fills me with a sense of possibility thinking. With each breathe, I release and let go making room to discover more fully my gifts and my potential so that I may serve others in the fullest capacity possible.

I inhale the brisk breeze as if taking in the nurturance of our planet earth. I feel renewed, strengthened, and powerful to create the dreams that swirl within me. With my fear released, I create room for greater possibilities, more opportunities and more individuals to share the essence of a joy-filled life.

As the breeze becomes cooler, I wrap myself in my blanket cuddling my own spirit, comforting my own sense of self, nurturing and resting.

With each whip of cool air, I feel a release of the imagined fears, the questioning "can it work" sensations and I remain open to the messages that the angels and God bring my way. Feeling empowered to forge ahead, I awake with a renewed sense of understanding that during this year it is time to act, time to create, time to share, and time to complete the writings that have been given to me. Now is the time to be fully me, one who will transport individuals from "I can't do it" to "I CAN." Now is the time to act. I inhale the brisk breeze of this morning and carry its power within me. The wind carries this message: It is time to create the vision stored within my soul.

✎ A New Vision

I hear the roar of the ocean calling my name;
I tighten, I fear—
My mind swims in the thoughts of what frightens me...
My heart says venture ahead—
My mind says I can't...
My heart says I can!

I hesitate, contemplate...
a wave approaches me—
I feel the power of the wave;
the steadiness beneath my feet;
the pounding of my heart—
I risk; I move ahead;
I embrace the wave—

Swish...in a moment, a short moment—
It's gone...the old vision...
the masks, the boundaries, the fears—
the limits wash away with the tide...

A refreshing freedom appears...
A newness of life,
A calm, a strength to face the challenges ahead,
A healing, a loving feeling...
Swish...in a moment, a short moment—

the limitations are gone...
the healing begins!

A moment in the waves of the ocean,
washes away the past and welcomes the present...
a moment to play, to rejuvenate, to renew...
With each wave, power is felt...positive energy is given...
unlimited potential is found!

Swish, a moment in the waves...
a message is given, a prayer is answered,
peace is felt...
a moment in the waves...
a new vision is gained...
look, it took...only a moment!

✎ Let it Snow

The snow pelts the windows, the wind howls, school is closed and the children squeal with joy. Gazing out the window, the wind swirls the snow like a painter swirls her paint on a tapestry. Cozy in front of a fire, the warmth of family and hot cocoa takes away the reality of the bitter cold day. Larger snow banks, cars spinning out of control, creating a necessary adjustment to one's overbooked schedule.

The excitement of the weathermen on TV "warns" others of the dangers that loom outside, increasing fear of those who live in the "fear space." Worry sets in about relatives near and far. Energy is spent on the concern for a flight that may or may not take off. Children seem to fully understand the gift of living in the moment, of adjusting to nature's ways. "Mom, can I go build a fort?" "Mom, can I ride the 4-wheeler to a friend's house down the road?" No concern for the bite of the wind. No concern for the treacherous travel. No concern for others in their journey…just pure joy! Joy for a "day off" from sitting in a hard chair at school, for taking another quiz, for listening to a lecture again. Yes, children seem to understand best how to flow with the changes of the weather.

Watching the news suggests very few flights are available. A "state of emergency" is called. "Stay off the road" is heard on radio and television.

Uncertain of whether my flight would leave, I waited to pack until the morning. 4:00 AM is now here and I'm ready to launch. Peering out the window, the world is white, sky and earth meet, swirling snow and snow banks form as one. Time to travel for the day. Embark on a journey to empower others to put "students first." Reconnect with a friend of long ago. Time to begin a journey of possibilities. My mind swirls with thoughts of hearing the news that the airport is open, yet wondering how it can be as I notice that the howling of the wind made the view out my window a solid mask of white.

With a courageous heart, I journey out the driveway and discover the roads are well-plowed; even the New York State Thruway is bare. I relax to inspirational music and realize that in a few hours I am going to be in Texas. Even though I find an unplowed airport parking lot, I maneuver to the gate for an on time departure.

A passenger is fidgeting nervously as the runway is covered with remnants of ice from last night's storm. With my eyes closed, I picture my day as I desire. A smooth flight, a reunion with a friend, an inspirational training the following day. Breathing peacefully, I am jolted out of my seat by an abrupt stopping of the plane's take off. The pilot says "we had to abort our take off due to blowing snow and will have to de-ice again and try later. You can use your cell phones at this time." Wow. It took nothing but a moment to turn an "on time departure" to a "we have no idea when we will take off" flight.

Hearing the frightened women in front of me talk to her loved ones from a space of fear, I realized that I was in such a peaceful state; I didn't realize what did happen. I chose not to go into the "what could have happened" imagination. Surrounded by individuals who were calling loved ones and telling them that they love them, I realized that so often we go through life without making the connections that matter most. I offered praise for the talent of the pilot, gratitude for the man in an open bucket truck who was de-icing in frigid temperatures, and thanks for all the flights that are on time. I was surrounded by individuals complaining about the airline, the delays, the antiquated de-icing machine and anything else they could grumble about. I noticed the dance of a snowflake on the window and imagined that my connecting flight would be delayed too and life would adjust accordingly.

We eventually did take off safely. We did experience delays with our connections and after 16 hours, we landed in Texas. In waiting, I noticed and listened and released all the challenges. I heard the laughter of a young child playing with a spoon. I experienced the patience of a soon-to-be husband working with an airline representative to find a connection to get him to his wedding on time in Mexico. Instead of being filled with anger and fear, I opened to the nuances of a day challenged by winter weather and I was blessed to experience resilience of the human spirit.

As I left the airport in Texas, I felt the warmth of the sun on my face. With no snowflakes in sight, I smiled.

✤ After the Storm

The sky glistens with magenta rays peering behind the blackened cloud. The sun sparkles beneath the clouds, yearning to reach beyond the storm that moments ago sent crackles and booms throughout the sky. Pausing to inhale the beauty of a serene sky, I remember the moments in life when an event or a situation transformed my life from a peaceful journey to a turbulent, unsettling experience.

An hour ago, life was normal with a heavy mugginess that is common in upstate New York in August. The sky was full of puffy, cotton candy clouds and within a few minutes, a flurry of wind swirled among us. People ran, scurrying for cover. Isn't that so with life? We sometimes are traveling through when unexpectedly something happens and our world turns into a storm? A loved one in an accident, an illness that isn't explainable, a business agreement that goes wrong or a quarrel that isn't resolved. Sometimes, we become so involved with the storms of life that we forget there will be an awakening after the storm, a newness of hope that will emerge.

I look out again to the horizon and the angry sky has transformed into hues of pink nestling against a light blue sky. The rain stops as instantly as it started. The darkened clouds transform and the sky is filled with a milieu of purple, pink and white. Raindrops cling to the windows as a reminder of the storm that traveled through, yet beyond the reminders of the storm is the promise of a new path. Rumblings are heard in the distance as the storm travels.

Sometimes in life we hold onto the memory of the storms of life. We hold onto the darkness after the journey. We hold onto the frightening internal trembling that arises when the uncertainty of a path is present.

Instead of accepting that the storm will pass and that much of what happens in a storm is out of our control, we cling even beyond the turbulence. We fear for what was and we bring it into new experiences. FLASH, the lightening that had subsided reappears. Just when you feel safe to venture forward, FLASH, another sign of the storm, hesitancy enters and then a vibration of confidence emerges when you look in another direction and notice a radiant sunset sliding down from the sky.

In life, we sometimes to forget to look in a new direction, consider a new solution or connect with another person. Sometimes we focus on the darkness of life's challenges instead of the opportunities that lie within the unexpected. It is simply in remembering…remember that storms pass; a new day begins. It is remembering that as the earth absorbs the tears from the sky, the grass sings for nourishment, the trees and flowers dance in the wind as they quench the relief from the humid day. It is remembering that to the campers and boaters, this storm is a challenge, and to the farmers and gardeners, this is an answer to their prayers.

✎ Forgiveness

Have you ever had a challenge with someone and hours or even days later you are still replaying it in your mind? People seem to spend so much time holding onto challenges from days gone by. They have an interaction with someone and it remains within them after the time spent. When interacting with people who may not understand your words or actions, remember to surround yourself in light and to also offer unconditional love and forgiveness to them. *How can I do that? They hurt me!* may be your reply to this suggestion of simple forgiveness. Yet holding on to the challenges creates "energetic ties" to their stuff. By embracing the idea, the highest good for all can occur in simple interactions. Forgiveness releases one to heal and allows everyone to consider the highest good for all involved. Forgiveness releases and opens. By wanting to change people, we break the ability to live in peace and harmony. Changing others suggests we "know" what is in their best interest, that we have the answer, that somehow we are in control. By allowing others to be who they are and for us to be who we are, an ebb and flow occurs, a dance of energetic harmony allows others to rise above circumstances, to transcend their current perspectives, to discover their solutions, to create healing within. By holding others in the wave of unconditional love and support they feel our light, our healing, our compassion, our positive energy. Wellness-emotional, physical, spiritual-it is all possible! The ripple of uncertainty, frustration, and wonderment can all be released and it becomes easy to open ourselves to be all we can be and desire.

✌ The Swirl of Turbulence

Challenging decisions . . . breathe.

Burden on your heart . . . share with another.

Let go of assumptions . . . discover the answers.

Open yourself to healing; feel lighter.

Solutions emerge quickly and goals are met.

Stay in the present moment.

Let others have their own experiences and discover your own next step.

Embrace what was and what can be.

Uncover the pain and discover the healing light.

Trust others in your life; you will no longer doubt.

Imagine that there is enough to fulfill all desires.

Invite openings into your life-walls crumble. Darkness lifts.

Trust your faith; the path ahead is guided for you.

God is with you to help you see a new way—a clearer possibility.

Let go of struggle and certainty abounds.

Grow into your DREAMS stored within your soul, easily achieved with an open heart.

Be vulnerable, be passionate, be true to your dreams.

Allow others to be who they are meant to be.

Ask and let the light in.

Embrace faith; be open to a sense of hope.

Forgive your friends. Let them live their path, their truth, their light.

Quiet your mind and listen to the voice of God.

Quiet the chatter of doubt and assumptions

Embrace the path ahead... in the quiet you will hear and understand.

Peace is your Gift.

✎ Oversize Load

Turning the corner, encountering a long truck carrying a wide solid concrete block, I found myself sighing at the idea that on this country road, I would be burdened with this obstacle in front of me. I found myself slowing down as he crept up the hill and gingerly varied his speed according to the terrain. After a few minutes, I snapped out of my resistance to this vehicle and realized that I could spend the next 30 miles wishing he would turn or I could surrender to the moment and stop focusing on the unsightly block in front of me peering through my window as if to say "I am in control here!"

Instead of focusing on the object, a large concrete beam that would be used to offer support for a bridge, I considered how we can create an internal bridge from where we currently are in life to where we want to be. We can stay focused on the challenges in our current path or we can consider that the very experiences that are frustrating us in the moment may be the ones that offer the grandest personal growth opportunities. How often do we become fixated on the obstacle rather than considering the opportunity that is hidden within this moment? I glanced away from this booming beam and I began to scan the horizon and discovered beauty I might have otherwise missed. To my right, cows grazing on a peaceful countryside, to my left, a pumpkin patch speckled with a variety of orange and a few curious seekers searching for just the right size and shape. The scene of young children with grandparents gleefully celebrating the picking of the pumpkin with the backdrop of a bursting forest of maples and oak trees would have been missed. Instead, I breathed in the beauty of this autumn day noticing the birds flying in V formation, working together as a team to reach their destination, an American flag proudly standing in the middle of a cornfield, patriotism at its finest, and a farm equipment store with their polished green and yellow tractors reminded me of the patience and determination each farmer shares to grow the vegetables we eat.

Sometimes in life we concentrate on the challenge of the moment for so long, sometimes hours, days and months after we have experienced it that we forget to look beyond knowing that an answer may be within our own reach. By fully embracing the problem and attaching to it, we don't leave room to reach out to the solutions.

Once I let go of the attachment to the idea that this oversized piece of concrete was going to slow down my day, I rediscovered the resilient spirit of our universe. The truck in front of me presented an opportunity to slow down and notice the world around me, not the destination in front of me. As I looked to each side, I marveled at the reds, oranges and yellows of the trees blowing in the wind and reaching to the heavens. I chuckled as I noticed the white picket fence adorned with little plastic pumpkins and leaf garland. The essence of joy seemed to vibrate from the yard. I wondered who played on the swing set.

I look ahead again and this time I notice the flight of a butterfly as it weaved above and around the concrete column. I laughed as I considered how simple the dance of the butterfly was and how easily we could dance through life with the spirit of a determined soul finding our way around or through any challenge on our path. Just then, a butterfly soars toward my windshield as I winced at the "attack." I imagined the butterfly laughing at the sight of my face as I squished my nose in concern for the butterfly. She probably just said back to me, "Remember it is about how you ride through the journey of life!"

The truck turns and I am "free" again to travel on the open road. This time though I look ahead and all around. I notice a truck with the letters CFI on the side and wonder what the initials stand for, and then I conclude "Clearly Following Intuition." This is my message for today and the gentle whisper of my internal wisdom would say "fly through life with the ease of a butterfly exploring its world; look beyond the challenges of the moment and realize that answers are all around us if we take a moment to look and listen."

Transforming Obstacles Into Opportunities

✎ Act Now

Overlooking the grand St. Lawrence River, sitting in the USA, and watching a boat pass the Canadian shoreline, I was capturing the glorious vibrant colors of the sky. Hues of pink, purple, red and orange, I was thankful for another day. The colors created patterns in the sky as if painting a moment in time for all to see. A sunset, that will never be experienced exactly the same again in this masterpiece of artwork, reminded me of the power of one day. Sometimes, we think and don't act; imagine the dream and let it rest within our heart instead of creating it in our world.

I arise to a new day, the brilliant yellow sun rises above the river, and another day is given to take this journey on our dream path, to make a positive difference in this world, to rejoice in the gift of life. I drink in the power of the new day, the sun warming my face and the warm breeze gently brushing against my body, knowing that I will soon leave this vacation spot and begin a new school year. Feelings rejuvenated by nature, filling my body with the peace of the river, my thoughts are interrupted by a neighbor. "Aren't you from Central New York?" "Yes," I reply. He continues, "It was hit by a horrible storm, a possible tornado and is in a state of emergency." How can life be so different just a few hours away? Just a short jaunt down the road, people are suffering, people are challenged, and people are not able to relish the glorious sunrise that I am experiencing.

A few phone calls later, I discover that my home is safe, escaping the dangerous path of the storm, and I also realize that many are not as fortunate as I was on this particular day. For some, they awoke to the aftermath of a destructive storm, mourning the loss of a loved one, or facing the devastation of their damaged home or business.

The message is clear for me: ACT TODAY. Pursue my goals yet not fulfilled, contact a person and tell them how they made a difference in my life, make a choice to appreciate the little gifts of life.

Take time today to reach out to someone and touch their life.

Take time today to let someone know you care.

Take time today to begin the journey of a new goal.

Take time today to thank someone who has made a difference in your life.

Take time today to hug a child.

Take time today to call an old friend.

Take time today to thank God for your blessings.

Take time today to create a new experience in your little corner of this world.

Share a smile with a stranger on the street.

Share a kind word when you feel gratitude in your heart.

Share a moment of silence for all who have gone before you.

Share a story with a little one or listen to someone in need.

Share yourself with the spirit of unconditional love.

As I listened to the news of the destruction, I consider that in ONE MINUTE life changed. Imagine if we used our "one minutes" with more passion, more commitment, more awareness for the influence we have on others. Imagine the possibilities if just one person used one minute to care for someone in need. Imagine if the one minute turned to five minutes, then one hour, then one day, then a week, a year. Imagine if we all lived life with the understanding that today is a gift. ACT NOW.

∽ After the Attack: September 11, 2001

This evening as I sit on the deck listening to inspirational music, my heart sorts through all that has occurred. The wind jostles the candles that I lit hours ago. They stay alive, determined, committed to be the light. One morning and our world is forever changed; a decision made by a small group of people to terrorize our lives. A brilliant blue sky turns to darkness that stirs within our hearts. We look up to the brightness of a shining star, as silence covers the earth. Just a few hours down the road, burdens are heavy, hearts are in pain, and a city is searching and searching.

A song on the radio reminds me of the healing that can emerge. "Can you feel the love tonight?" The flicker of candles dance in the darkness, the butter-fly chimes create a melody with the kiss of the wind. A flame is blown out by the wind. It is gone, yet the vision remains, the light is in our heart, memories embraced within one's heart. The quiet sky lights up with a passing plane high above the horizon. In the silence, crickets harmonize creating a melody that fills the essence of this moment. One golden star shines brightly. Delilah on the radio plays *Count on Me*.

The wind silences and the candles reflect across the deck resembling the rays of the sun. I look to the west and think of the joy of the summer. I look to the east just a few hours down the road and feel the heaviness of my heart for all who mourn. I look above and ask God for strength. My children rest peace-fully. I wonder about parents who lost their children. A shooting star zip-zooms, across the sky. One candle remains lit, projecting its light outward as if reach-ing the unreachable. I sit alone, yet feel the presence of many. I imagine a circle of love and remember all who remember loved ones tonight. The radio shares "when a hero comes along…there's a hero if you look inside your heart…there's an answer if you reach into your soul; it will melt your sorrow…"

Restless sleep filled with racing thoughts and "what ifs" swirling in my mind, I wonder if our world will ever be the same. I question the quality of life. I toss and turn with ideas of how to support others. I wonder if people will release judgments and unify in support of those who mourn and those who seek messages about their loved ones. I surrender that God has a plan for our country, our world, our Universe. Something great will come from this tragedy.

The next morning in our corner of upstate New York, life proceeds "as usual" as we prepare for school until Mike comes down the stairs. With his favorite little action figures in hand, rescue workers, an ambulance man and a police man, he speaks with wisdom beyond his just five years old.

"Mommy, can you mail these to the firemen in New York City?"

"Tell me more Mike."

"Well, I know the firemen are looking for their friends and they are sad, so I thought if I sent them my toys, they would feel happy again. They can take time to play with these while having their lunch."

As I swallow and hold back the tears that I am feeling for the "knowingness" that is displayed by Mike, Tara (age 11) enters the kitchen. With enthusiasm and foresight she says "Mom, I was thinking how my friends and I can show our support. I want to get safety pins and red, white and blue beads and make a symbol that we can wear on our shoes to show we care. Can we go to the store after school and have friends over and make enough for the whole grade?" I smile and with tears of appreciation for my children, I reply "Yes, we certainly can!"

The simplicity of a gesture of kindness, my son and daughter reminded me that the world will be better. People will connect with the pain of others and reach within their hearts and discover how they can support. With simple acts, genuine, heartfelt connections, our world will grow bright again. As we honor those who are called to act, called to respond, called to rescue others, called to serve, let us be the light in our own corner of the world. Let us carry hope in our hearts, vision in our minds and peace in our soul.

✎ Angel's Landing

A vastness of possibilities lies within me as I consider the next steps in this adventure called Life. A serene sense of self emerges as I awake with knowingness that life has much to offer and I have much to discover. With each breath, I remember the essence of an experience that was created for me. After a powerful weekend with women who dream and wonder about their own capabilities, I discovered the power of focusing with one's inner intention and one's inner strength. With each step, I inhaled the beauty that surrounded me.

The majestic mountains call me. The inspiration overflows within me. The cherished moments with a genuine friend empower me. As my mind remembers, my spirit knows that with one breathe, with one step, you can become closer to creating the magic of your dreams.

When I first saw the mountains of Zion National Park, I was filled with a spiritual sense of wonder and inspiration to believe that so much is possible. Dreams seemed bigger as I gazed at the towers of rock and meandering road. Amazed at all that stood before me and wondering what would unfold next. I began walking on the switchbacks. Feeling like a little kid experiencing the world for the first time, noticing the vegetation and trees that found a way to grow between rock crevices, I considered the moments in life when perseverance made all the difference. Towering sheets of rock surrounded me and as I walked further, my heart rate let me know that the elevation was changing and a memory of my first climb flooded my mind. With memories swirling and reassurance that the next ledge was yet a better photo opportunity, I continued.

With each turn, I climbed higher and higher, at times with muscles saying "Ouch! I haven't been used in a while." Magically, the path changed and we were between two walls of rock with greenery everywhere. Trees budding forth, finding their inner strength to grow, finding their connection with the earth reminded me of how humans have the capability to find their way through life's challenges. Stopping and looking at a terraced path, I realized that dreams are a layering of experiences where one moment may have an impact on another moment, where one person's comment can help transform a life by empowering an individual. It is as if life gives you what you need to help you in your transpersonal discoveries.

As I continued along the way, I took deeper breathes of air. Climbing higher with a gentle breeze swirling, I became centered and in awe at the views that I was breathing into my spirit. It was as if the energy of the rocks was filling my soul and recharging the spirit that allows others to transform and become more of who they are meant to be. Looking at the breathtaking beauty that I have never experienced before, I considered what other opportunities are available that I haven't yet discovered. Wondering what lies ahead, what possibilities emerge when one comes from a place of certainty and inner knowingness, I quiet myself and embrace the possibility of a dream.

With each step I was pondering the essence of living, the power of remaining true to my gifts. Feeling blessed by the connection of friendship, I simply became fully present noticing the color changing in the rocks, the crystals of sand on the rocks, and the blades of grass that find their way to the surface. I wondered who thought of creating this path and how they did it. I feel certain that others said "it couldn't be done" and probably they doubted themselves, yet one person or maybe many decided to allow the beauty of this park to be shared with millions. One person's dream touched my life today. One friend's kindness allowed me to experience the greatness within that I know is there and sometimes forget to notice.

My swirling thoughts stopped when I saw people coming down a HUGE rock formation that looked like only a few inches wide suspended high above the earth. "How did they get there?" I ask myself. At first, doubt and uncertainty entered my mind, even though I knew I wasn't going to fall and take the ride of my life down the side of a mountain, yet it was still there. Dreaming BIG replaced those thoughts. *Remain true to self* resonated within me. I took a moment to breathe in the beauty that surrounded me, majestic mountains all around me. A surge of energy seemed to resonate from the earth. I inhaled. With each step, I felt confident and playful, pulling myself up on the rocks and finding the way.

Contemplating each moment, I wanted to savor this gift. Noticing the changing colors as the sun began its descent, I began the climb step by step, seemingly suspended above the earth and feeling one with the universe. Connected to a source that was greater than me and at the same time seemed to resonate from within me, I heard God speaking to me. No longer did I notice the sheer drops of the cliffs. No longer did I feel a sense of "what am I doing up there?" No longer did I wonder if dreams are possible. I know they are! I possessed a sense of inner contentment that will remain within me always. Periodically, stopping and inhaling the beauty around me, sensing a connection with spirit that was swirling in my body, and feeling a oneness with mind, body and spirit, my soul seemed to sing. As I moved across the narrow saddleback and began the ascent to the top, I looked back and saw where I traveled from. I was in awe. What else is possible in life?

Step by step, dreams begin to unfold. Sometimes in life we don't know the next turn or the next piece of the dream. Sometimes it seems scary not knowing how something will unfold and the solution may be just around the corner, the next bend in the mountain climb of life. At times I laughed thinking "no way" and then would feel the inspiration of the universe around me.

Atop Angel's Landing, the view was incredible in all directions. Surrendering to the power of the universe, to the whispers of the angels, to the connection of heart that I feel, I breathe in the beauty of Zion National Park. Trusting the gift that has been given to create programs that transform lives, I dream with an inner peace, a love of life, and a contentment of spirit.

When I take a moment to remember the climb, I am filled with tears of pure joy for being fully present. By allowing one's light to shine in the world, lives can open to new heights, create new experiences within one's self. When we allow ourselves to quiet the mind, we discover our inner source of strength and inspiration. As I breathe in the pictures in my mind of "Angel's Landing," I realize there is so much potential yet to unfold. There is power within the dreams, seeing how high I climbed, it seemed almost effortless at the hardest points. Nearing the pinnacle, an inner joy was felt that set my spirit free. No expectations, no responsibilities, no confinements of spirit.

As I sat on top of the mountain, my spirit was free. My soul connected to those who have gone before me as if I hear them whisper their messages that left an imprint on my soul. Isn't that so true of life? We can live fully each moment, connecting and embracing those who cross our path or we can fill our minds with limitations, our hearts with doubt, and our spirit with burdens. We can allow our light to shine so that in the silence, lives unfold, spirits renew and connections strengthen between strangers who may only share a moment in time or strangers who become friends on the path of life.

As we walk through life, and consider that the path we are on is the one for life or we may explore further to discover there are many paths, many possibilities, many hopes and many dreams. In a moment, you can close your eyes and remember the experiences that seem to transport you to another place, filling you with a sense of majestic power within your being.

As the sun sets and fills the sky with a brilliance of purple and pink hues, I realize that an experience can leave a savoring imprint on your soul that will transcend time and space. As the sky darkens, a light is noticed in the distance. As the full moon peeks over the mountain top, its power radiates the spirit of potential. Honoring the gifts that are stored within me, I give thanks for the whispers of wisdom that I possess, knowing that when I share my special gifts, when I allow myself to just be real, to be "me," those who cross my path seem to light up. Visions that capture the essence of living that others may never see or experience are opportunities to create experiences for others that will allow them to seek their truth. By being fully present and creating a safe space for others to unfold and renew their spirit, the ability to heal, to see within and to hear the wisdom of their souls emerges into the light. As I inhale the beauty of the experience of "Angel's Landing," I trust the dreams as they unfold. I imagine that all that has been given can be shared.

Gratitude for this experience fills my heart. This experience is a gift, a remembrance, a completion. Once again, closing my eyes and inhaling the beauty of this mountain climb, my heart is filled with love for the moments in life when heaven and earth connect, when the unexplainable transpersonal messages of the spirit resonate within me, and when the gift of friendship creates an experience that is such a message from the heart. Feeling blessed by this experience, I allow my heart to fill with gratitude for an experience that transcended far beyond the rocky path, beyond the moonlit sky, and beyond the paths that I walk, step by step by step.

❧ Looking Beyond

As I drive to the 6:00 AM yoga class, heavy dark clouds loom overhead creating a barrier to the glorious blue sky of the day before. There is no evidence that an endless sky filled with a tapestry of blue existed the day before. As people awake this early morning, they are greeted with layers upon layers of black clouds, with various shades of gray and somber white speckled throughout. Some might even groan *another dreary day in Central New York* as they greet their morning.

As I walk into the fitness center, I feel a warm breeze kiss my cheek and sense that today would unfold magically and open to wonderful possibilities of sunshine. At that precise moment, I can look up and notice the layering of darkness or I can look around and embrace the simple signs of spring: daffodils pushing through the ground, a robin searching for worms on the field, or the unfurled earth awaiting the planting of a butterfly garden. Yes, in one moment, I can transcend what some might consider as the possibility of a rainy day unfolding or I can look for other evidence that it is a sleepy morning waiting to blossom into a day filled with opportunities to notice that life is unfolding all around us.

In life, we sometimes allow one interaction, one medical report, or one unexpected turn of events to consume our entire day and we miss the sparkling moments along the way. In life, we sometimes hang on to what was or we worry about what will be and we miss the inspirational moment that greets us when we stop and ponder the opening of a new day. When we stay focused on the problem, life still moves all around us and we are remiss in experiencing the beauty of a day, noticing that the sky moves, the earth rotates, the birds fly and the trees bend in the wind. When we stay focused on the problem, we aren't noticing the people that enter our path in our journey of life who may be able to provide a solution that hasn't yet been considered. By focusing on the challenges, we remain separate from our truth. It is in removing the layers that we discover our truths.

As the yoga class begins, I commit to releasing all that takes me away from the present moment; the *to-do* items on my list, the tasks of the day, my concern for others, the planning for the projects and the other zillion things that seem to enter and swirl around in my mind. As I choose to center and breathe deeply, an opening within occurs and washes away that was, all that might be, and all that can be. With each new breath, I discover that all that is around me no longer exists in this present moment. Opening, releasing, connecting to the inner light that lies within each of us invites the transformation of the new day to begin.

As I look out the window at the dark sky, I realize that we can remain fixated on the "dark clouds" of our life or we can remember that there are solutions, discoveries, and possibilities as our gifts. My mind transports me to my last flight, when our plane was high above the clouds and we were experiencing a brilliant sun and crystal blue sky with clouds below us, yet people below were looking up at the layers of clouds. From high above, we saw miles of stretching sky at the same time that individuals heading to work were experiencing the barrier of clouds, forgetting that the crystal blue sky may actually be the gift of the day.

Almost on cue, when this realization entered my mind, I noticed that the clouds began to separate and patches of blue sky peeked through the heavy blanket of clouds. The first noticeable opening resembles a heart. Yes, the opening to the sky above was in the shape of a heart. I breathed deeply. I contemplate what life can be when we lead with our heart, when we share compassion for others, when we connect at a level that trusts others and releases judgment. As we stretched our bodies, anchoring our feet firmly into the floor with our focus ahead, I realized that when we are fully present in the moment, the world seems to float around us just as the clouds in the sky were passing by as the earth rotated. When we stay in the power of the moment, forgetting what was and letting go of what will be, we notice that the "clouds of life" float by, that the moment of frustration that we are experiencing will soon pass, the due date will soon be a memory, and the challenge of the day will only have the power that we give it. When I stay in the power of a moment, I notice another opening in the clouds above in the shape of a heart, a little larger than the one before, yet it is a heart. Breathing deeply again and looking ahead at the possibility of the day unfolding in a way that I desired, I stand firmly and watch the clouds float away, another opening, in the shape of a heart, and another and another. I blink, thinking my mind has entered a zone of unreal dimension, and as quickly confirm that the sky is speckled with openings in the shapes of hearts. A scene from childhood enters my mind remembering a hot, summer day when I lazily laid on the grass and looked up at the sky, playing "what do you see?" I imagined the elephants, horses and dogs in the sky. Today, I create a new game of "what can be?" and I gaze between the now separating clouds and I discover beyond the blocks, experiencing the gateway to the solutions that seem to "show up" when we move beyond the apparent "problem" in our life. Paying attention, staying in the moment, the joy that I was experiencing for my discovered heart, I realize disappears as quickly as it came. The earth continues to rotate and the clouds swiftly continue their journey.

Isn't that so of life? We can be fixated on a problem that we experience in our day and carry it along with us in our journey of life. If my mind remained focused on the early morning clouds, I may have never noticed that the sky was giving birth to a new day and that the openings of blue reminded me to live with heart. In one hour, the day became totally different, yet how often do we look out the window, draw a conclusion of what the day will be like and then match our mood to that precise interpretation? How often, do we see the obstacle (the clouds) instead of viewing the opportunity that lies between the challenges of life? How often do we forget that we have a choice at every moment of creating perceptions for life experiences? I continue to breathe and stretch, feeling renewed, refreshed and empowered. In one hour, my life has transcended all that was before me when I awoke. By focusing on the openings, the power of a problem diminishes. By focusing on the light that was creating this day, the layers of confusion, doubt, worry or concern are whisked away with the clouds. By focusing on the unfolding of a new day with all the gifts it can bring when we remain open to the blessings, life becomes a joy to live.

As the clouds move rapidly by, I glance once more to the sky. In one hour, a dreary sky has given birth to a blue sky speckled with clouds. A large blue opening reveals the shape of a butterfly with the wisps of clouds forming its antennas. Yes, to live with the freedom of a butterfly in flight, with the love of an open heart, and with the determination of a bud on a tree pushing through the branch, so it can take the form of a leaf. Yes, to notice the magic of nature in one moment in time, this is truly transcending all that surrounds us. Beyond the challenges of life, we can fully embrace living in the moment.

⬧ Beyond the Fog

Driving down the highway, I notice the hillside marked with trees and the silhouette of clouds that darken patches of trees, making it harder to see the blossoming autumn colors in Upstate New York. It's morning. The sun is rising and the day is beginning once again. As I dip into the valley, the hillsides are no longer visible. The fog envelopes the trees and the mist gently raises from an almost invisible river. The picturesque hillside has disappeared into the embrace of the fog. Thick, heavy, white clouds mask the horizon.

Pondering the essence of fog in one's life, I consider how we sometimes allow challenging moments to fog our ability to discover the possibilities hidden within the problem. We temporarily focus on the mask of challenge that seems to present itself. We even forget that moments before we may have been able to resolve the situation, yet we become immobilized with fear or uncertainty and we carry a burden within us, masking our reasoning ability. Our thoughts swim in our mind at a time when we just want clarity. Our heart forgets that the answers lie within and we see only the cloudiness of our decision-making ability. I wonder how much time is actually spent "in the fog." If only we would surrender to the moments when life becomes confusing, truly understanding that we have the ability to resolve all challenges.

Yes, the fog disguises the countryside yet it doesn't take away its beauty. Just as for humans, it only creates a mask. If we are patient and resilient, we will unearth the solutions. Just as I consider the impact of a "foggy vision," I notice to my left that the sky is opening and the brilliance of blue is once again visible. The fog seems to float away into the atmosphere and the vibrantly painted autumn trees are again in sight. Rust, orange, yellow and browns are sprinkled amongst the evergreen trees and remind me of the resilience of one's soul, the power of one's determination. Just a few months ago, the trees were barren and now they are filled with colors and in just a few weeks the leaves will soon drop onto the earth's carpet. A cyclic rhythm of existence reminds me of the ebb and flow of life; the journey that we all explore when we see beyond the fog.

↝ Sparkles after the Storm

The raging winter storm alarmed many and kept people inside as the treacherous driving conditions challenged even the most experienced North Country driver. Events cancelled, schools closed, and neighbors shoveling a path to the road created grumbles in the air. People complained about the inconveniences of the chilling, blustery day.

Yet a day later as one arises, the sun shines! The sky is blue. The snow sparkles as if each individual snowflake is shouting "look at me." The trees glisten with snow-covered branches and icicles hang from the rooftops. Nature has painted a new picture in the woods behind my home. The landscape takes on a new feeling, a breathtaking orchestration of individual snowflakes connecting to create a blanket of powdery cover. The trees look fresh and renewed instead of barren from their lost leaves; the snow covers the hill and awaits the laughter of children on their sleds, and the sparkles on the snow resemble the radiance of diamonds.

As I look out my window, I imagine that life is much like the weather outside. When we are in a "storm" in life, we often see the obstacles and we struggle as we ponder. *When will this "storm" ever end?* Instead of discovering the opportunities hidden within the storm, we worry the day away. We forget to look out the window and notice that the soft snow resembles a dusting of angel sparkles, gently creating a powder of hope on top of a crusty frozen surface reminding us of the layering of possibilities above the challenging moments.

Creating time to explore the freshly covered earth, I decide to bundle up and cross country ski. Staying on the known trail, yet yearning for the unknown, I take the less traveled path, uncertain of the destination, yet intrigued by its quiet unruffled snow.

Feeling one with nature, the sounds of the woods quieted my spirit, creating a protection around me. As I traveled further from the known, I discovered new scenes, open views and a resilient spirit. My joyful heart took chances, captured a moment by following a hunch, traveling off the groomed trails to uncover a meandering trail in the distance.

Skiing down a very steep hill, safe yet uncertain, I journeyed through the Glen. Now it's time to climb, higher and higher. I remove my skies for the upward journey. I find freedom in being able to choose how to explore, and pause to embrace the beauty of the moment. I notice how the snow hugs a fallen tree and watch in amazement as a squirrel jumps from branch to branch, scattering snow droplets onto my jacket.

It's a delightful 17 degrees; a welcomed change from the minus 21 degrees yesterday. The "warmth" of today invites people out to explore and I cross paths with both young and old alike, all out to capture the gift of nature, to connect with the crispness of a fallen snow. The sparkle of a single ray of sun reflects on the snowflakes. The light can radiate in our lives just as the individual flakes of snow connect to form a blanket in the wilderness.

Connections create a tapestry of joy, fluffy elements of peace, and a silence that transcends world challenges. It reminds me that the softness of a snowflake gently coasting to earth can transform our focus, our attitude, and our joy. And, during the next storm of life, we can be assured that the sun will once again rise and offer us a new perspective.

❧ The Mist of the Mountains

"It's misting again," exclaims my son Mike as we embark on another piece of our journey. Time together in the mountains, only to have the weather pattern limit our hikes and our exploration of wilderness, we explore other possibilities. As he examines the tiniest of rocks that adorn the yard, I gaze in the distance to a mountain range that captures the attention of many who ponder the trails. Today, it is socked in with heavy, dark clouds. Today, the tips of the mountain are not visibly connected with the blue skies. Today, the gray skies kiss the tops of the trees, sending a message of "leave me alone" to those who gaze at its beauty.

Remembering the brilliant autumn colors, speckles of orange, rust, yellow and red, a snapshot memory seems to lighten the darkness. Remembering the brilliance of a ball of sunshine radiating on the green leaves that blossom in spring, a snapshot memory seems to enter my mind and I imagine that the cobalt blue skies are really just hidden behind the thickened clouds.

Gazing again in the distance, I consider the times in life when decisions plague inner light, when uncertainty clouds one's focus or when problems create heaviness on one's heart. I wonder if it is really about lifting above the current perceived challenge that we feel the brilliance of the sun, and feel like we can reach upward toward our vision, our dreams.

When we look upward into the sky, we can discover that we are able to travel further than we originally thought we could. When we reach the top of the mountain and gaze around at the breathtaking beauty in the distance, we wonder why we felt any concern for the steep steps that we took along the way. We remember the deep breaths as we transcended the slope, yet we instantly forget as we gaze in the distance at the majestic mountains and the rambling brook.

✧ Through the Rain

The sun glistening on the trees warmed the autumn colors. The vibrancy of the reds, oranges and yellows touched my heart with a warmth of the transformation that our earth goes through each year. Tears welled in my eyes as I felt the luster of color from the very branches that were dancing in the wind. I had been on this road many years ago and I was touched by memory as I recall the laughter shared with friends as we meandered down the curves of a mountain road. In a moment, the majestic radiance of the sun kissed the trees and melted away any concerns of what will be or what was. Time momentarily seems to stop as I inhaled the beauty of the trees delicately planted on the side of a mountain enduring all kinds of weather and staying firmly grounded in their presence.

As the drive continued, the rain started to pelt the windows and within time the torrential downpour and the darkened sky made it difficult to even see the tree-lined highway. I recalled the moment when I embraced the joyful dance of sun-kissed trees in the mountain and I realized that no matter what problem we face, no matter what circumstances we face, we can endure with the strength of a mountain tree. As I considered the power of nature and the connection of heaven and earth, I realized that just as quickly as I focus on the rain, I can focus on looking beyond the rain. Once I changed my focus to think beyond the rain, I started to notice the silhouette of birch trees intermingling with the maples. Even though darkness now enveloped the earth, a hint of memory of the resilient trees remained within me.

No longer was I mumbling about the storm. I was offering gratitude for the rain knowing that rain and cool nights creates the vibrancy of the trees that only an hour earlier had brought me great joy. No longer was I concerned about the rain pelting the window. I quieted myself to hear the repeated pattern of the rain as it created its own symphony. No longer was I noticing the darkness; I was imagining the animals in the forest, the hikers on the summit, and the farmers thankful for the rain.

By changing my focus, I uncovered the beauty of the storm. By remembering an earlier joy, I began to search for a glimmer of a colorful leaf, still in the forest, yet not quite visible to the human eye. By creating a sense of knowingness for the symbolism of a storm in our life, I realized that so often, it is due to a storm that we unearth our truest colors. It is often after we have endured a storm that we plant firmly into our sense of *beingness*, trusting the journey.

✢ With the Spirit of Childhood
Dedicated to Tara and Mike

As I notice his mud covered hands,
I smile and realize he created new pathways for his trucks.

As I view all the picture frames on the floor and notice the empty shelves, I smile and realize she is a promising interior decorator in action.

As I watch the snow fall out of his boots,
I smile and realize he jumped through the snow.

As I see the bottles of paint lined up on the table,
I smile and realize that creativity is brewing.

As I spot the tub of Lego's dumped on the floor,
I smile and realize he discovered the one special piece that was missing.

As I notice the shaving cream all over our yard and driveway,
I smile and realize the genuine connection of a father and son playing together.

As I watch my daughter invent a way to luge down our driveway,
I smile and realize that courage is abundant and joy is self-created.

As I discover the scotch tape container is empty again,
I smile and realize it helped create a mini-skateboard park.

As I see the tiny pieces of black foam board on the carpet,
I smile and realize it is the remnants of a six foot Abraham Lincoln creation.

As I open the garage door to find piles of wood,
I smile and realize a new half-pipe is going to be constructed.

As I witness the frequent moving of furniture in my daughter's room,
I smile and realize that there are many ways to design your space.

As I listen to the enthusiastic cry "it's snowing, let's go build a snowman," I smile and realize that life is about playing when you get a surprise storm in October.

As I remember the moments, I smile and realize that living with the spirit of children allows us to rediscover our playful, creative and resilient selves.

Exploring
New Dreams & New Pathways
to Self

✎ Renewal Moments

As I awake from a nap on the deck, I realize that the last few Sundays have been days to refuel and reconnect with my spirit. As we go, do and accomplish, it is also important to take time to just "be." It is a time of renewal when we allow our minds to wander into the dream space, the zone that creates without boundaries, considers without limitations, and feels the essence of truly living in the moment. With each connection, a life can be changed; with each task, a goal can be reached. With each action, a step closer to the actualization of a dream can be taken. So often, we dream and not act. Consider and allow the imagined limitations of our mind that prevent us from creating all that we can imagine. Relationships, jobs, contentment, time to enjoy nature, laughter with family and friends, opportunities that just begin "showing up" when we are open. Time to consider that if we live with heart and lead with heart, we begin to feel the wonder of this planet, the transcendence of time between friends near and far. We can be a part of the ripple of love and light that others carry within their hearts when we decide to truly show up as people who care, people who dream, and people who allow others to matter in their own way. With their own hopes and dreams. No longer do we operate from a perspective of *they should, you might want to,* or *you have to.* Instead, we open ourselves to divine light and love, magical moments, ah-hah experiences, glimmers of nature speaking to us, through us and around us. Some call it God's love, some say radiant internal energy. Others label it divine light. A stranger in the store, a child on his bike, a face in a crowd, all in need of warmth, unconditional regard and welcoming support, open themselves to solutions when we consider for a moment that we may be the conduit, the vessel, the vehicle to support others, move others, and connect with others. Letting go of their outward behaviors and seeing their light especially, through their darkness, the boundaries they create to protect themselves from pain, memoirs, or hidden challenges. When we let go of the preconceived notions of what must be and open ourselves to what can be, we center and renew ourselves to connect on another level. Life is opening to new possibilities.

I feel the knowingness that the journey is unfolding just as it is meant to unfold, capturing a feeling that I am in the exact place I am meant to be in. I renew my spirit knowing that with each setting, a lesson can be shared. I understand that with each human interaction, a story can spark a new idea. I trust that with each smile, warmth can be felt, and with each spirit a light can be brightened.

It is time to step into the new dream, to create the new adventure, to discover my true path. I find comfort in knowing that others too can create their own experiences, learn their own lessons and embrace the possibility of a new day and a new dream. It is time to live in the spirit of light and love, to honor the divine energy that is available all around us, to create a moment in nature to connect and touch with the spirit of the earth. Lessons will unfold, people will come to guide and support, and answers will be discovered within. The power exists within to create, connect and consider the smiles when others "get it," laughter when others relax with who they are, tears when others release the blocks that hold them back and light when others connect in the magical world of the invisible forces that guide us along the way.

✤ The Dance of a Butterfly

Sitting in the wilderness, I watch the dance of a butterfly. Fluttering with grace, from flower to flower, it reaches its destination, seeking nourishment and resting spots. It dances with a sense of conviction to reach that spot, unconcerned with the challenges that surround it, just flying, seeking, understanding and trusting it will arrive.

Dancing with the dream that all will be provided for; it glides with the wind, allowing the wind to carry it to the next resting spot. Soaring high and low, in and out, it continues with confidence seeking its outcome. The butterfly opens and closes its wings with a free spirit of joy. Dancing with the ebb and flow of the wind, it graces our path filled with courage and determination.

Just days ago, it was a furry caterpillar squirming along the ground, perhaps uncertain of its path, unaware of the obstacles that inhibited its full growth. Someone walking could have easily terminated its life; someone could have limited its potential. Yet, today when the butterfly soars, it remembers only the journey of hope and passion.

Isn't that the way life is sometimes? We have experiences in our past that limit who we think we are or who we think we can become and then a particular moment, an interaction with someone, or an intuitive insight that we listen to invites us to emerge with the strength of a butterfly in flight.

We can spread our wings, expand our influence, consider the possibilities of a journey ahead where all will be provided, all will be discovered, and all will be revealed. It is in trusting the journey that we really live, that we fully participate in the cycle of life as we listen to the whispers of wisdom that nature provides.

It is in slowing down long enough to notice a butterfly in flight that the concerns of yesterday seem to evaporate into the wind that is supporting the flight of the very butterfly that we are gazing at. Surrendering to the whisper of wisdom that surrounds us always yet escapes us often, we unleash the power that is within us, the power that allows our dreams to take flight, our passions to soar and our convictions to emerge as real connections from one human to another. Surrendering, trusting, believing, acting with intention to make a difference in this world, it is then that we soar with the courage of a butterfly dancing in the wind.

⊷ The Dream, Dare, and Dance Journey

We open our hearts and uplift our spirits, inviting a joyful journey of inward exploration into our lives. Pausing from the world around us, we make a commitment to ourselves!

We breathe out the challenges of days long ago and embark on a new journey… Loved ones hug us with the fabric of unconditional love and light. Discovering our inner strength, our spirit soars; our vision expands of what is possible.

We open to new messages, new discoveries and new paths to explore. We rekindle the resilient spirit and become the captain of our destiny. We open our minds, our solution-creating energy sparkles and solutions emerge effortlessly.

Whispers of intuition gently guide us on our path. Our creative spirit designs the future that our heart calls forth. We embrace the hidden potential that emerges when we dare to dream.

We open our spirit, our heart's joy sings, our real self dances with a lightness of spirit. We open our soul, we discover that we are all one, walking a path of discovery, dancing with our dreams and weaving peace, love and joy in our world.

We dream, we dare, and we dance our own personal journey…

↬ Remembering the Light

As I look around the forest, I see so many paths, so many directions, and so many possibilities. I stand among the trees and at times feel the darkness from the tasks that block me from the light. I look up and see towering evergreens, majestic maples, and thickets of brush. All around me beauty; all around me choice. As I walk further into the forest, I let go of the expectations of others, the challenges of a day. Step by step, walking, discovering, and listening to the brisk breeze that kisses the trees. Taking a moment to be silent, to surrender to the placid sounds of nature, to notice how a leaf bends one way then another as the wind passes by. Sensing the scurry of the furry animals as they find safety from the unknown sounds of the day, remembering that even the tiniest ant "knows" what to do; the earthworms "know" how to form a path within the dirt, and the tiniest of bugs discover their home within a tree, "knowing" that the match feels just right for their needs.

I stand, surrounded by the tallest of trees, noticing the paths as they spin off in so many directions. I ponder the next steps, not seeing the final path, perhaps not even understanding the pull that I feel to explore in so many ways. Standing alone, deciding, wondering, listening....no longer to the voices of many, to the "please help me, no me, no me" and finding myself swirling around to meet the needs of many. No...standing alone, listening to the beating of my heart, to the whisper of the wind, to the unheard messages stored within my intuition. Standing alone, yet feeling connected to so many, to their needs, to my needs, to many paths. Looking around at the forest at so many options, and so many opportunities to serve, to use my gifts, to empower others, and to embrace the light, I consider the many paths available to me. Seeking clarity, wisdom, divine light-listening, acting, serving, and trusting that with each step insight will shine forth. Spinning around as each day presents a new possibility, a new path, and a new solution. Looking, feeling, connecting, and no longer running away from the possibility of the larger dream, I realize that each moment is part of the creation of the greater purpose. Each decision, each interaction, each awareness brings clarity to the path ahead. In the silence of intuition, I hear so many voices, so many needing my gifts, wanting my talents, feeling my energy. With each challenge, they feel I have the solution. With each struggle, they ask me to serve. With each problem, they seek healing from me.

Step by step, I let go of the *should do's* and *have to's* and I discover that the light within will lead me on the path that is part of my journey, safely creating the outcomes along the way. Sometimes, there are other paths off the destined one that will curiously grab my attention, seeking me to follow its direction. "It is just a little bend, come with me around this corner, it leads back to the main path," calling, pleading, wanting me to follow its way. It is safe, known, and comfortable. It is serving others, part of my calling, part of my gift, yet it is also unknown, uncertain, and unpredictable.

Looking around the forest again, I begin to see between the trees, I hear what isn't said, I feel what isn't touched. I connect at a deep place where intuition and thought connect, where integration begins. I feel what others are thinking; I see what is invisible to the human eye; I touch without being physically present; I think in ways many have yet to discover. The darkness of the forest begins to shine with a brilliance of light that seems overwhelming, seems more than I have ever experienced before, and seems certain. That is right, not uncertain, rather certain, familiar, known.

The path that I travel is leading me to many new experiences, all part of the plan. Lives intertwine with mine at just the destined moment. Events interrupt the "scheduled, planned out" day at just the perfect moment. What seemed like interruption is actually all part of the plan to re-discover the light that shines within, to reconnect to the flame that is meant to help others in their journey of life, to heal, to unfurl, to discover their potential.

Listening to the requests of many, sometimes feeling their pain so deeply within my heart and sometimes hearing the swirling thoughts in my mind so loudly, I begin to connect. Begin to connect with the divine light that is within each of us. I begin to remember…to remember that the light of one can connect to the light of another, transcend time and space, heal from afar, support from a distance.

As I consider the opportunity to take a bend in the path, to journey down a side road in the forest, the wind picks up; the moment is disturbed by uncontrollable, unexpected twist of events. Within a few minutes, the wind howls, the rain horizontally pelts the windows, the dark clouds roll in. Within a few minutes the dawn of a new day becomes turbulent, ripping trees from their grounded roots, cracking majestic trees in half, toppling them onto homes, roads, and lawns. Within a few minutes, this corner of the world becomes interrupted. As I watch from the window, I consider for a moment that the journey is NOW, the dream is NOW, the decision to write, to empower others in NOW.

As I stand in the forest, I feel no fear; I feel no uncertainty, and no turbulence within. The turmoil of the weather anchors me in my dream, grounds me in my path, and allows me to fully experience the connection of mind, body, spirit. The confusion all around me no longer permeates who I am or who I am meant to be. An internal connection radiates outward, as I trust and listen to the whisper of my own internal breath, the discovery is made, easily and without hesitation.

Serving others? Yes! By serving myself, by expressing my needs, by taking my own path, I serve others. I empower others to believe more fully in their dream, to take action to follow the light of their path, to uncover the solutions stored deep within their heart. I empower others to see a new perspective, to give another person an opportunity to grow, to learn, to serve on their path, their destination. I empower others to realize that many have gifts yet discovered, talents waiting to come to life. I empower institutions to consider another way, another path for their students, their faculty and their community.

Yes, by integrating the desires of my heart with the thoughts in my mind, I remember to allow the divine light to shine forth in my thoughts, in my words and in my deeds. I become the light that heals, the light that serves and the light that enables others to realize that all they need is within them. Solutions emerge, unique opportunities open up, and connections remain.

The paths in the forest are many and in life when we stay true to our purpose, allowing our vision to clearly speak, it is then that we discover all we need is being provided for us, when we listen to the whisper of our dreams. When we step firmly on our path, we notice the other meandering paths in the forest, yet we continue step by step knowing that each challenge, each unexpected storm is actually a gift helping us grow and see clearly with a higher vision. People enter our path, teach us lessons, steer us off course sometimes, and by giving thanks for the interactions, we become firmly rooted in our essence, trusting that those who remain will guide us along the way. Anchored in our dreams, we feel the storm around us, yet it doesn't permeate our being. We hear the wind slap against our dreams, yet we stay within the comfort of our knowingness that the light will be shone to us, the solutions discovered and the impact will be larger than we can ever imagine.

In the quiet of this early morning, there is no visible wind, no seemingly distracting choices, no uncertainty, and no puzzling decisions. There is only peace, love and light within and around. There is a sense of calm that surrounds me and grows within me. Step by step, staying "on course," knowing and trusting that all will be provided to create the dream that is confidently emerging from my heart, I continue my journey. It begins with each interaction, with each thought, with each connection. The path will meander, the faces we meet will be diverse, yet the outcome will be the same. The light radiates in the forest, dances through the trees, sparkling for all who enter on the path. When we stay true to our life's purpose, people will discover their light, feel the light of others, and spread the light in the world.

⭗ Parallel Paths

The inner whisper prompts me to take a drive. My detailed, schedule-oriented mind shouted "what are you thinking? You have things to accomplish, things to do, things to achieve." As I continued working on the items on my to-do list, I continually was interrupted by the message to go to Hamilton, New York. "It's only a short drive and perhaps a story will unfold" was the balance to my "No, don't go" restrictions in my mind. I pause from the pre-scheduled day and open up to a journey.

As I breathe in the beauty of the awakening of spring in Central New York, I realized that sometimes the tasks of the day take our focus away from nature's breathtaking essence. As I drove down the road, I noticed the blossoming of a multitude of green colors gently popping through on the barren trees. Just a week ago, the landscape yearned for color. Brown fields, brown trees, a reminder of the sleep of winter and today a moment of rebirth, so many shades of green joining together to create a unified field, a reminder of the strength within. Light green, olive green, emerald green, earth coming back to life after a cold winter when the earth lies dormant. Reaching for the sun, feeling the warmth of the iridescent sky, the leaves reached openly and effortlessly. I imagined life could become as alive as the rebirth of spring.

I wondered if we took a moment each day to connect with the simple process of nature if we would feel renewed, strengthened and empowered. If we took a moment to notice the world around us, would the energy that brings our horizons back to life also renew our spirit? The road meanders, twists and turns. Our forefathers had a destination in mind when they created this country road. In and out around the natural features of our planet, they created this road that now is home to farms and country living. A speckling of houses dot the horizon where cows and horses gaze, even one little colt yearns to grow strong.

In the distance, I see a home canvassed with tulips. Every spot of earth is covered with yellow, red, purple, pink and white. As I drive by, an older woman appears at the door. I give her a "thumbs up" and a smile for the beauty she created and her wide grin lets me know she felt my gratitude. A split moment of beauty remains in my heart just by noticing the blossoming of spring. Some may notice the older structure of her home, badly in need of repair and others focus on the beauty of flowers that stay vibrant if only for a few weeks. Isn't that so with life? We can focus on what needs repair or we can focus on the beauty of a moment. We can wallow in the items that need attention or we can grasp the beauty of a flower waving hello in the wind.

Sometimes we stay on the same course, follow the same paths in life and other times we risk to see where a new path might lead. I wondered about the path that the "tulip woman" journeyed in life. I wondered about the choice she made to decorate her yard for others to breathe in its beauty. I wondered where the car ahead of me was going…so I turned as they turned. I laughed at the simple choice to follow a new course, journey on a new path, and as we took various turns I wondered where we were headed, never having been on this road before, yet somehow trusting the journey. When we came to a fork in the road, I laughed, realizing that we were on parallel paths during this journey. We were heading in the same direction; the strangers in front just knew a shortcut! I chuckled as I realized that in life we sometimes don't take the chance to discover a new course, a new system, a new way. We sometimes follow one course thinking "it is the way" and find ourselves dismissing the suggestions that others share. Sometimes we head toward our goal and we think we are on the right course, yet there may be an easier way to get there, an easier system to use. By opening up to new solutions, we discover more of what we want in life. We embrace new beginnings, we welcome suggestions.

We allow ourselves to trust our intuition to take a journey away from a prescheduled day.

Today, I choose to look for the blossoming of spring, notice the wave of a tulip in the wind and the connection of the sun's rays as it supports the growth of the leaves, opening to another season of shade and spring-time fun. Today, I choose to find my answers by pausing for a moment on a blue skied spring day, by taking a new parallel path and discovering more than I even know at this moment in time. What will you notice today? What will you experience today? The swirling to-do list in your mind or a gift of nature that leaves a heart print in your life? You really can have both and more than you ever imagined.

↬ Pathways

The road is winding, the way is a challenge…
Two paths may you go.
The first is rough, with a mountain of uncertainty,
The second is smooth, with a horizon ahead.
One fills you with fear, and the other with hope.
Which one do you choose?

Never alone, guided and protected along the way,
Gently nudged when we doubt or worry,
Trusting we can find our way…

Reaching, seeking, believing,
Dancing when the storm comes,
Feeling beyond the pain…
Seeing the possibilities…

My friend—choose to walk with faith and the road ahead will be a journey…
filled with love, peace, and contentment.

✎ Why Do They Tell Me?

Why do they tell me to go another way?
My heart blossoms with love, the glitter in my eye,
The future is unknown; there will be struggles on the way.
My love increases daily—how can they tell me to go another way?

I begin to crush the fears that cloud my way.
I possess hope and desire my faith grows each day.
Do they really need to tell me to go another way?

Uncertainties fill my mind; insecurity plagues my day.
Strength is the answer, to be found on the way...
They need not tell me to go another way.
I have the power to dream the finest dream,
To see the grandest star and to be the happy me!

Will I go another way? That is yet to be seen, but for now, I'll be me!!

Appreciating
Angelic Moments

✎ A Gift from the Ocean

An early morning walk on Myrtle Beach proved to give me a gift of the heart. As I reflected on the journey of life wondering about the experiences of the year, the loss of John, I gazed outward noticing the rhythmic pattern of the waves. As if on cue, the waves lapped against the shoreline. As I stood at the crest of the ocean, allowing the waves to gently brush against my bare feet, I noticed a seashell different from the rest. I picked it up only to find a hole in it. I then thought how often in life we judge people and circumstances as "less than" instead of finding the inner beauty of the experience. We sometimes see something we desire, but then judge it as less than worthy and we do not embrace the possibilities that may be hidden within its outer shell. Couldn't we just patch the holes in life and in the lives of others?

Upon further examination of the shell, I discovered that the "hole" was actually in the shape of a heart. As in life, sometimes our greatest challenge actually becomes our most wonderful triumph. Sometimes with many aspects of life, we miss the opportunities, the moments to connect. Just as I was pondering the insights about life, the ocean jolted me as a huge wave brought in shells and pulled many away. I started looking for other shells, other messages, yet even though I could see them in the water, as soon as I went to grab some, they would be pulled away just as quickly as they came.

That is how life is…a fleeting moment to make a difference in the lives of one or of many, and we find ourselves preoccupied with daily chores. Sometimes we consider making a difference and we remain still instead of acting, instead of creating our dreams. Then, in a moment, the opportunity has passed, washing away like a wave kissing the sandy shore.

Sometimes, our focus is on the outer appearances, the outer behaviors and we never discover the "inner" shell of a child. We don't discover the heart or soul of a person. How often in life do we hold onto an idea that could touch the lives of others? How often do we hold back when we could touch the heart of a stranger or a loved one?

Just as one wave gently brushes my feet, another pulls me further in the ocean, tossing broken shells against my bare skin. As one wave caresses, the other pushes away creating a reaction to retreat. Isn't that so in life? One gentle nudge, one connection will empower us to act and then a tumbling of broken shells, broken lives will bring us into retreat formation. What if we don't reach? What if we don't seek? What if we don't touch the lives of others?

As I glance again at the opening in the shell, the heart carved out by the kiss of the ocean, I remember, John, a mentor, a colleague and most importantly a friend who conversation by conversation inspired me to be more than I realized I could be. I thought about the hole in the hearts of all who loved him. I considered what he would want us to do now. I realized it was time to create the dreams stored within our hearts. Just as the seashell entered my path today, its message can enter the hearts of others. With each moment we have an opportunity to discover the hidden treasures stored within each person. With each moment, we have an opportunity to re-examine our perceptions as we look at the challenges in life, the holes that we want to repair. With each moment, we have an opportunity to rediscover the heart of the message that may be hidden within the holes of our lives.

✎ I Am the Wind
Dedicated to Loved Ones Who Left Before Us

I am the Wind, Carrying Away your Confusion…
I am a bird perched on a tiny branch,
discovering my inner strength.
I am balance within that allows the challenges to diminish.

I am the Wind, Carrying Away your Sadness…
I am the swirl of light that emanates from the sunrise.
I am rain that melts away the fear.

I am the Wind, Carrying Away your Challenges…
I am the swan, the dance of elegant grace.
I am the sunset that stretches across the horizon.

I am the Wind, Carrying Away your Troubles…
I am the breath that balances from within.
I am a smile that brightens your day.

I am the Wind, Carrying Away your Guilt…
I am the leaves that sway in the breeze.
I am the butterfly that dances from flower to flower.

I am the Wind, Carrying Away your Fear…
I am the invisible energy of a hummingbird.
I am the wisdom that discovers answers.

I am Joy within your Laughter.

I am Love that shines within your heart.

I am Peace within your soul.

I am Resilience within your spirit.

I am the Wind....

✑ Millie's Music

A simple moment can leave an imprint that transcends our existence in that time and space. Simple conversations shared around a kitchen table fill us with enduring lessons. Being fully present for someone as they share their concern, giving without thought of return, noticing if someone is in need, and finding a solution to help may appear as simple actions, yet they leave an imprint on one's heart. Meeting as strangers and becoming family through simple gestures of kindness is the result of living your life filled with joy. Laughter during the card game *Pitch* or generosity of vegetables shared from a garden creates a connection from the heart. Stories swirl within our minds; lessons remain long after the interaction takes place, and the essence of the person is carried within our souls.

A kind word shared with another human being may bring light where there is challenge, solutions where there is confusion, or peace where there is turmoil. A compassionate listener who puts aside their needs to be there for another may offer just the needed advice that brings calm to a hurried day.

As I listened to the stories of Millie Champion Hibbard, a mosaic of music was heard within the stories that individuals shared. This symphony of kindness was created by her simple interactions that touched people's lives. It was evident that the simple moments made all the difference. Sharing a fresh piece of homemade pie was an offering from one neighbor to another that became a connection from the heart. Noticing the young boys riding the bikes back and forth on the sidewalk and offering a glass of water carried a smile from one generation to another. Conversation at a kitchen table seemed to alleviate the tension in a life. A few phone calls to friends to generate a solution for someone in need became the beginning of the bond of friendship to a newcomer in the neighborhood.

As we journey through life let us remember that it is the simple moments that add sparkles to our day. It costs nothing, yet reaps great benefits. It takes only a moment to share a thank you, offer a helping hand or be fully present for another in your life. I invite you today to reconnect with a friend, reach out to a stranger or bring joy to others who enter your path. With Millie's spirit, let us embrace the sparkling moments of this day!

✎ Serenity

One day an image of serenity came to my mind. I shared this with a friend and he asked what it looked like. I was unsure how to answer. Sometimes in life the feelings that resonate within our being are often intangible. Describing them as specific actions or behaviors is often challenging, yet exactly what our mind craves. If we know what it looks like, we can experience it, right? Yet, from my own self-discovery, I have learned that often the gifts that are most special are ones we experience when we become centered within. When we create a space of unconditional love in our hearts, we begin to experience the world in a new way. Challenges can be all around us, yet we see the gifts in the moments. People can become invigorated with resentment and turmoil and we can radiate peace from within. By allowing our minds and our egos to rest, we open to the fullest potential that resonates in a magical place deep within our being.

It is with nature that we discover serenity. It is the sun's rays that sparkle on a lake. It is the splash of rainbow colors as the sun kisses the horizon at the end of a day. It is the snow dancing across the yard, gently carried by the wind, reminding us that so much of life is invisible. The wind is invisible, yet powerful; unseen, yet guiding; unnoticeable yet present.

We are like the wind. Our spirit is an essence that others can feel and yet not even realize they are feeling it. Our intentions seem to vibrate around a room even though it is not recognizable. Our thoughts create an energy that connects with the energy of another and forms a connection that is often unexplainable within our own awareness.

We are like the sun as our light can shine and brighten the darkness in one's life. Our light can heal without ever saying a word. Our light can create peace without ever mentioning a thought. Sometimes others may feel our spirit, our light, our essence and it creates uncomfortable sensations within their being. Sometimes we feel another's energy that creates uncertainty within ourselves. It is the gift of serenity that allows us to transcend the moments of a day.

So…what does serenity look like? It is the acceptance of people for who they are at any given moment. It is letting go of expectations and assumptions, so that we become open to the messages of our inner wind, the whisper of our intuition. Serenity is a sense of being grounded in a world of chaos, being open in a world of minds that are closed. Serenity is the connection that comes when light and love emanate from our hearts. Serenity is offering gratitude for the experiences of a day, even if they wear the disguise of challenge. When we are open to receive, we gather our life's lessons.

Serenity is a spirit of inner contentment, an awareness of all the ah-hah moments of life rolled up into one interaction, and a space that protects us from others who may not have discovered the inner peace that we can emanate to the world.

Serenity is created from within, from breathing deeply and from capturing the sparkles of a day. A smile of a stranger, a giggle of a young child, a kindness shared between friends—any experience when your heart smiles and your mind relaxes, allowing your spirit to guide you along the way. Serenity is hearing the howl of the freezing cold wind on the outside and smiling because you are experiencing the warmth of your own internal fire on the inside.

⊹ The Gift of Song

The long-awaited phone call came; one I didn't want to acknowledge its arrival. "Your dad has little time," resonated in my mind as I heard my mom describe his failing health. It was the Tuesday before Christmas. I knew that when I saw him on Saturday that it could most likely be the last of the times I shared with him. I wanted to pretend that the scene I experienced wasn't real. I wanted to think about the molasses cookies he requested from the recipe that I hadn't made in years. I searched just because…dad asked!

Mom asked me to come and my mind raced. There were lesson plans to create, holiday cookies to make, anything but the inevitable reality entered my mind. I thought I would drive in the morning. I returned to school to make some lesson plans, tie up loose ends before I left for a parting that surely would be imminent. As I drove to school, I recalled the navy whistle he found in the box hidden deep in his closet. This whistle that he blew in WWII as a young sailor created a song in his heart on the last day that I saw him. I remember the grand smile, the essence of inner joy, as he grabbed his breath after creating a few notes significant of this call, stepping aboard the journey of a lifetime.

As I sat at the computer and wrestled with the appropriate lessons, I heard rustling of the feet in the distance. I looked into the hallway and saw the young ladies and gentlemen dressed in their holiday attire. Ah-hah! The holiday concert was today. What a great reprieve from the reality of the moment. I left my office, walked down the hall, and took a seat in the back row.

The music jumped off the walls of the old auditorium, the last concert before the renovation project began. As I listened to the harmonizing voices, the snapshots of time gone by entered my mind. The shy sixth graders during my first year at this school, now seniors, were receiving thunderous applause for their talents. A young man insecure as a 7th grader now confidently sings a solo. This special group of students joined together to create a spiritual harmony. I felt surrounded by angels and just pretended it isn't all happening.

When the song *Oh, Holy Night* began, I recalled the times when I listened as a young child to the chorus in my hometown. I remember the holiday concerts that my family attended; the joy in the eyes of my dad as he listened and believed in the words.

As I absorbed the music into my being, I transcended the stress of the impending death of my dad. I released the inner turmoil that I would hide during the work day. I purely listened to the joy of the teens sharing their talents, of teens willing to activate their joy of music and connect with their audience.

I felt the atmosphere change and love filled the auditorium. I felt the burden of the days to come lifted from my being. As Elena sang, *Oh, Holy Night*, I felt a sense of peace surround me. I left the concert renewed and ready to complete the plans that I needed to before I traveled north.

I slept deeply during the night and abruptly woke at 4:00 AM with the voice of Elena singing *Oh Holy Night, the stars are brightly shining, it is the night of the dear Savior's birth*. At 6:00 AM, I was dreaming of Elena singing, seeing her on the stage as a confident, talented young lady. I was startled by the ring of the phone. I jumped and answered and heard the words. "Your dad died at 4:00 AM, peacefully, and...." My mom's voice faded.

A new journey would begin, but the gift of peace created by the song would always be with me.

✣ The Light of Love

Driving down the highway, I contemplated the lessons that John had taught me. Smiling at the memories and shedding tears for the moments I missed to tell him how I felt, I looked at the sky searching for an explanation, wanting to make sense of it all. Squinting at the sun, it was an unseasonably warm day for early December in Central New York. The sun melted on the horizon and seemed to guide me as I listened to songs on the radio… "I will remember you…You'll be in my heart…" I tethered between a heart filled with sadness for the loss and a heart filled with blessings for the opportunities of friendship and mentoring that I received from John.

The orange sun filled the sky, blossoming vibrantly. As I gazed to the right of the sun, I noticed a cloud shaped like the wings of an angel, so much like an angel that I grabbed a piece of paper to draw the sight. Awed at the moment, I was filled with the belief that John was a dear angel on earth always giving without thought of return. Quickly the orange sun faded into hues of purple and pink. The sun filled the sky with layers of radiance; the angel cloud faded away, and the sky began to darken. As night was drawing near, the candlelight procession would soon begin.

Children, teachers, Little League parents, veterans, business owners, and church members, John touched many lives in this little town. Wondering how many people would be joining the procession, I imagined the love that would be felt in this place John called home. The darkness of the sky separated by the purple glow stretched over the town. The clouds parted and another cloud emerged, one circled by the blue sky and in the formation of a cross. It wasn't time for the stars to appear, yet a star did appear just as I was entering the small, peaceful town.

The young and old were pouring out of their cars, all meeting at the parking lot of the funeral home. With lit candles, we proceeded to John's home. The glow of the candles filled the street and step by step we walked in silence. Suddenly, a large gust of wind blew out hundreds of candles and we joked about how John's spirit was blowing them out, not wanting to be the center of attention! As we walked, the church bells rang, the wind howled, and the flags stood at half mast signifying the difference that one man can make in a community.

His family stood in awe as they silently offered gratitude for the people whose presence offered a tribute to John. Without prompting, someone began singing *Amazing Grace* and many joined. Others stood in prayer. I remembered an Eskimo legend that guides us to believe that stars are openings to heaven so your loved ones can look down upon you and fill your hearts with comfort. Just then, we noticed a light shone brightly over their home, a bright star, the only visible one in the sky. People looked and looked, yet no one saw another star. Feeling a nudge from the wind, I went forward, extending my hand to Christine, John's wife. I brought her to our group so she could see the star. I pointed and said, "He is with us—in our hearts." Christine looked up, cried loudly, and collapsed in my arms. One by one, other family members came off the porch to see the guiding star. Ever so gently, as if on cue, other stars began to speckle the sky, a reminder for us to live life the way John did, reaching out to others and committing ourselves to go a little further.

I slowly and silently returned to the starting point, ever so often looking over my shoulder to see the bright star in the sky. When we reached our final destination, I looked again, only to find a sky filled with clouds. The stars disappeared, yet their message to share the light of love remained in our hearts.

The light of love is within our hearts to share at any moment. Once we experience the love of a friend, the light is always with us to share with others who cross our path in life. Events in life may dim our light, yet we only need to look up at the sky and watch the dance of a sparkling star and remember that we can share our light, our sparkling presence with others in the world. One by one, we can light up the world with our gifts.

⟡ The Sparkling Moments

Sometimes in life, people wonder how they will make a difference in this world. They consider new career paths, another degree, or putting more hours into their work day. We think "do, do, do" with hopes of achieving more, creating more, and earning the label of "successful" in the eyes of the world. Sometimes, the essence of life is hidden within the wonderment of a moment that is shared with another human being!

A simple moment in time can leave an imprint that transcends our existence in that time and space. The man sitting at the welcome desk of the hospital, wearing a funny hat, as I entered to visit a friend; the airline agent who managed to find a seat for me on an booked airplane after he answered "yes" to my question, "How would YOU like to be the person that creates a better day for me?" or the driver who shared his passion for the people he transports to and from the hospital. Simple conversations with enduring lessons. Sharing a moment with strangers who genuinely showed up in life as joyful, kind souls who live fully by their presence is a reminder of the power of one interaction. Their impact on my life remains within me, their stories swirl in my mind, their essence is carried within my soul, yet they may never realize the power of their simple gestures.

A kind word shared with another human being may bring light where there is challenge, solutions where there is confusion, or peace where there is turmoil. A compassionate listener who puts aside their needs to be there for another may offer just the needed advice that brings calm to a hurried day. Simple gestures of reaching out to others remain as moments in time that are carried within our hearts as we travel through life.

✎ Opening and Releasing

Wide awake at 4 AM, my body forgets to change over to PST time! Seeking a sunrise, I instead notice the darkness of the wee hours of this morning. Contemplating the desire to go for a run and realizing it is safer to wait until the sun opens the day, I consider what has been happening at Breakthrough to Success Training facilitated by Jack Canfield. Being with individuals who yearn to live life to its fullest, I hold them in the gentlest light trusting that the answers they seek will emerge from their souls. Joyful for the positive energy of this experience, I offer gratitude for this day. Outside lightness begins to peek into my room.

With my IPOD strapped to my arm, I invite Fred Johnson's inspirational music to fuel the possibility of running effortlessly (a new talent I am discovering). Noticing all that surrounds me, I ponder the ripples in the water that the gentle early morning breeze provides and I consider the ripples that we are all creating in the lives of all who cross our path. With a simple smile, a kind answer, a sense of purpose and a open presence, individuals open and release what holds them back. Running, contemplating, discovering the ocean and remembering a day long ago when the ocean used to frightened me ever since being caught in an undertow, I embark on a joyful journey. I remove my sneakers and embrace the dance of the waves and connect with the cool sand. Inviting the waves to wash away any uncertainty, I consider options for my future.

As I run, the freedom within dances as the wind kisses my face. What is the message of this morning? How can we create a space of unity, unconditional love and acceptance that will vibrate throughout our planet, allowing all to discover the deepest messages of their heart? Noticing something round in the sand, I pause and pick it up. Amazed that I am experiencing my first sand dollar, I am mesmerized by the details. I contemplate the power of God's creations as I examine the intricate details of this blessing. I contemplate the ability of like-minded individuals seeking truth, creating a ripple that transcends this moment in time. Noticing the tiniest of details, I feel warmth within my heart. As I walk, I feel a message emerging and I pick up another item. Tears begin to flow as the item resembles a butterfly, symbolic of my desire to feel the freedom of my dreams. Turning it over, it is actually three "broken" shells merged as one.

Seeking the emergence of the missing answers to my next steps in life, I feel the resonance of this moment. Little did I know this "butterfly" would be an instrument of healing for someone I meet later that day. As I continued my run on the beach, my excitement for the butterfly shell resulted in the cracking of the "perfect" sand dollar. Tears openly flowed as I was so certain that there was a message in this sand dollar and now it is "broken." I considered moments this year when I wondered if I could continue to pursue the dream that tugged at my heart. Gazing at the waves again, I walked into the water (just because I could on a November day) inviting the ocean to wash away the doubt that was entering my consciousness. I remembered a student from my summer camp, Megan, and her message. "Leaders for Life is a moment in my life when I was reborn into the person I always wanted to be!" I laughed at how quickly the doubt faded. Looking below, I noticed another sand dollar, and when I turned it over I saw that the other side was broken, yet I could see the intricacies of the its inner design. I reflected how during our "broken moments," we sometimes discover our truest essence. Without knowing what Jack planned for the day, I knew it was a day when others would open from within and release what no longer served them. And I felt that it would happen as quickly as the touch of wave to the shoreline.

Listening to the affirmation song that was designed for me by Fred, I recall the vision that it embraces and I smiled. I set the intention to discover another message for this day as the sun rises above the horizon to guide me. As I capture the message in my soul, I look ahead and discover another item on the beach...yes, a third sand dollar. This one is completely whole. Breathing with joy and crying with the excitement of what nature is providing for me, I embrace the essence of living and pausing long enough to notice the simple messages in nature. I realize the power of my book filled with inspirational stories will bring to people's lives.

I look above the ocean and a family of pelicans dances in the sky. As I enjoy my first experience with these interesting birds, I consider how our planet dances as one. Allowing one another to be who we are, blending our talents and gifts, trusting our unique abilities, we dance as one with the vision of embracing and expressing radiant divine love. As the pelicans dance in unison and flow above the waves, contemplating their next move, they seem to flow as one.

An awareness of the passing time snaps me out of my experience with nature and I put sneakers on and with the awareness of sand in my socks, I run with insights overflowing from my heart. Feeling that the sand dollar has a message, I discover that it is a spiritual symbol, representing Christ's birth and death. And, in its "brokenness" a legend suggests a release of good will and peace, a sharing of the gospel. I smile with joy and understanding in my soul for the work that is being created within the room I will enter in just a few moments. I embrace my faith and contemplate the essence of divine love speaking through nature this morning.

Poof. This moment on the beach fades from my memory and as I write on this November 16th morning, now 3,000 miles away from that California beach, I notice the dance of snowflakes outside my New York window. I realize how quickly life can change from a dance with the ocean to a dance with the opening of winter, yet in a reflective moment, I am back at the beach! I realize how quickly life can be transformed, how healing can occur with a simple sharing of a "butterfly" found on the beach. I realize how sharing a broken piece of a sand dollar is really symbolic of what we do when we join together. We come from many corners of the world and we join in spirit, in play, in love, and in joy and we commit ourselves to be of service for all who desire capturing the essence of living from the heart. The heart prints remain within every person.

With gratitude I acknowledge each of you for being who you are, for stretching to become more of your divine self, for trusting that all the challenges are part of the journey. And, remember, in a moment of brokenness it may really be an opportunity to allow goodness and peace to flow through you. When you notice something that is less than, allow the hidden treasures to emerge. When you contemplate your next steps, trust that you are surrounded by Spirit, supporting you and holding you with the intention of love and light. Connections of the heart transcend time and space and as you invite the message of this story within your heart, you can hear the slapping of an ocean wave against a shoreline, you can feel the crystals of sand in your hand and you can capture the essence of a sand dollar, when you pause...long enough to notice.

Creating
the Ripple Effect

✧ Living Passionately

It is in gently guiding others that we discover our true essence.

It is in allowing others to experience life without judgment that we discover our inner strength.

It is in sharing from the heart that we find a connection that moves others beyond where they are in the present moment.

It is in trusting ourselves and our friends that we open ourselves to possibilities that stretch beyond our current understanding of living.

It is in seeking goodness in all that we allow others to open themselves to healing.

It is in holding the highest intentions that we create an experience where boundaries are broken, insights are gained, and a giving spirit is felt.

It is in flexibility that we discover solutions.

It is in the strength of friends that we find our own resilience.

It is in our *beingness* that we feel the light of others.

It is during a calm focus that we feel the invisible transcending others to new heights.

It is from the support of caring people that we unlock one's potential.

It is in visualizing the possibilities that we uncover the creative forces that inspire us to believe further; to open ourselves to others and to serve the world with a loving spirit of kindness.

It is in opening our hearts that we create a ripple of love and light that strengthens others from within.

⤙ Living with Heart

As we move through the journey of life, let us embrace the possibility that strangers can become friends, that individuals can dream larger, and that a moment in time can create a sparkle within that moves others to believe. As you pursue the visions in your mind, the passion within your heart, and determination within your soul, remember that one interaction can make all the difference. As you experience life, I invite you to notice and share…connect and cherish…dream and act…

As you allow yourself to grow, take a journey with me and imagine…

Imagine . . .

> …a healing embrace
>> …a silent glance when one knows the essence of the inner message
>
> …a melting away of pain and suffering
>
> …an unfolding of potential
>
> …a dreaming sense of *"I can do it!"*
>
> …a sense of wonder
>> …compassion from within capturing one's fullest potential…unfolding…opening
>
> …stretching beyond the imagined limits of the mind
>
> …strengthening passion
>
> …a surrender of doubt and fear
>
> …an awakening of the wise one from within
>> …a recognition of others unlike ourselves who seem to have the missing piece to our puzzle
>
> …a connection of hearts
>> …a silent embrace of souls that whisper "I love you just the way you are"

...an intensity of purpose

...an unraveling commitment to peace

...a risk, a step toward our goal

   ...an unleashing of confined thoughts, of hidden memories, of broken dreams

   ...a strength, a fortitude, a removal of the barriers that once engulfed the dreams

...an opening to divine wisdom

...the courage captured in a story

...a silent whisper embracing the heart

   ...capturing a moment in time stored within one's treasure box in their heart

...a beating of hearts unified and connected to others

   ...future-oriented, solution-making principles, allowing one's greatness to shine

   ...whisking away the shame, doubt, and unfulfilled work to move forward to one's fullest potential

...a rejuvenation of dreams

...a commitment to peace, joy, and love

   ...a playfulness of spirits, a connection to one's inner child who dances freely, who laughs heartedly, who imagines fully

   ...recommitting to purpose, to love, to believing that in a moment a heart can be opened

   ...a boundary removed, a headache or backache released, planting seeds of hope and healing

   ...rebuilding the determination of a spirit connected to the divine

   ...knowing that people enter our path as orchestrated from above

   ...removing the coat of fear and covering your soul, body and mind with love

   ...seeking answers, discovering solutions, letting go of preconceived notions, limiting internal thoughts, extremely installed messages of childhood...

...renewing the faith, opening to love

...washing away of wrinkled memories, of the tension and turbulence of uncertainty and pain

...allowing the light from within to shine forth, smoothing the edges of pain

...seeking light to light, angels on earth—glittering angel sparkles fill the room

...embracing the night, forging ahead with conviction—the ah-hah moments...strangers becoming friends, releasing love and laughter...and *connections of the heart!*

᧞ Minnowbrook Memories

The kiss of the wind creates a vibration as it touches the earth. The ripple in the newly melted water creates a pattern of possibility. It gently nudges the ice covered waters to open with the connection of the warmth of the sun as it shines brightly on this spring day. The wind jostles the newly uncovered branches, no longer burdened with the shawl of icy snow, no longer buried beneath a drape of white covered earth.

Forward, open waters sparkle with the dance of spring. As the brilliant blue sky opens, a bird chirps in delight. The sun warms my spirit as I gaze upward breathing in the possibility of a dream. We are all connected.

The earth beneath me feels cold as I sit here inhaling the resilience of a spring day. The snow behind me reminds me of an unexpected storm just a few days ago. The radiance of the sun warms my spirit. Inhaling the glory of the moment, my heart opens to the sound of a babbling brook in the distance.

The wind snaps; its vibration becomes a symphony as it carries with it the kiss of the jostled leaves and evergreen needles. A small pine tree stands firm before me, grounded, rooted, growing where it is planted. The branches reach upward as if to sing the praises of this glorious day. The needles dance with glee as the invisible wind touches its spirit. Inner strength allows the tree to firmly embrace the moment.

Looking outward, a rock tossed into a silent lake creates a new vibration. The moving water gently kisses the shoreline while the frozen water in the distance remains solid suggesting that the water there isn't moving. Yet beneath the surface we know the dance of life continues. I notice an island, distant, yet connected; simple, yet majestic; alone, yet whole. An island standing on its own captures the attention of all who view the lake.

A magnificent lodge, quiet with the hush of memories, reminds me of the transformation that can occur within what seems to be just moments. As we transform the possibility of creating freedom within one's soul, we remember. Souls connected, understanding, embracing a moment in nature. Gentle footsteps in the distance suggest contemplation. A birch tree rekindles a memory of a day in childhood when transplanting a tree lead to failure yet now the birch tree speaks of success, of victory, of taking a chance, giving life to new opportunities.

The earth and sky connects—harmony embraced; love experienced. In the silence of nature, one's heart sings. Noticing a partial moon high in the sky, always there yet not always visible, like our inner peace, our contentment, our vision. Sometimes, we need to pause and reflect, rekindle the dreams within our hearts, remember who we truly are and who we want to be.

Our new perspective reminds us of the possibility that may always be there, yet not always recognized. As we toss a rock in the lake, we release what holds us back. We discover our resilient spirit. We open to new dreams, a new journey in life. As we breathe in the mountain air, we contemplate, surrender to what was, reconnect to what can be…this moment ends, yet the passion within our hearts grows.

As I look around Minnowbrook for one last glimpse, I realize that the lessons remain within my mind, the vision in my heart grows and the determination of my spirit flutters like a butterfly that has emerged from the cocoon of doubt and uncertainty. The sun sparkles on the water and the ripple of possibilities grows.

⊷ One by One

As we approach the later years of life, we often wonder about the journey that was, the experiences that were, and the wishes that might have been. What is exciting about life is at any moment we can remember that it is the simple interactions that make a difference. Listening to the whispers of our heart allow us to take action to make a difference in someone's day. By calling a friend in need, sharing flowers from our garden to brighten someone's sadness, and connecting with like-minded people, our thirst for knowledge is rekindled, our passion for living is enriched and our desire to continue to make a positive difference in this world is enhanced.

One by one, we can reach out and connect with someone in need, offering hope for the discouraged, courage for the fearful, or joy for the uncertain. We often journey through the "hurry" of daily living and we forget to recount the moments when a conversation brought a smile to someone in the hospital, a card brought happiness to a friend, or a home-cooked meal brought nourishment to a family in need.

It isn't the grandiose accomplishments that are needed. Rather, the simple human touches are ones that can be shared without cost and without hesitation. When we listen to the voice of our intuition and take action to reach out, we connect at a deep level…heart to heart. It is in taking action that we bring joy to ourselves and others. By letting go of the considerations, the doubts, and the worry about how the action will be received, we find ourselves free to be all we desire.

Imagine a world where neighbor helps neighbor, stranger says hello to stranger, young and old appreciate one another. Imagine a world where solutions are discovered by sharing "what worked for me was…" Imagine a world where we trusted who we are and who we are meant to be. Imagine a world where we awake each day feeling healthy and happy, committed to seeing beauty in the sparkling moments of a day.

As we journey in life, we can create many opportunities to serve. As each person connects with another, a ripple of love is felt. Just as a pebble tossed into a pond creates a ripple that vibrates throughout still waters, our simple actions remain long after the action has been shared. An encouraging word uplifts another and they feel better and continue by sharing a positive story with each other. With each individual, one by one, the energy of peace and love begins to be felt in one's home and community.

As you reflect on this message, may it renew your spirit, inspire you to reconnect with a friend, empower you to share an idea with another and remind you that YOU make a DIFFERENCE! Thanks for inspiring others!

↶ Genuine Love

"What did I feel?" This question entered my mind as I reflected the events of the evening. Hmm… "What did I feel?" An experience that was only beginning to reveal itself, the words seemed to escape me, yet the vibration of peace and love resonated throughout my being.

"What did I feel?" How often in life do we forget to allow our feelings to be exposed, to emerge, to release? How often do we take time to express to others what we store in our hearts? We meander through life with the intention of accomplishing tasks, achieving goals, moving forward with projects, forgetting to create a space in our lives to slow down long enough to notice; long enough to hear the messages stored within our hearts.

So often, we forget to pause and inhale the beauty of a simple act of kindness, to notice the joy on one's face as a radiant smile is shared between friends reminiscing of days gone by. So often we pass through a day without a second thought about the power of one interaction, one opportunity created to help another person grow. When we live in our heads, with the swirling thoughts of next steps, long-term goals, and wonderings, we miss the magical moments. It is in these moments that we feel a heart connection of two individuals whose paths crossed at a moment in time when one needed another for support, ideas, and to help them dream of possibilities. Sharing the gift of the whisper of one's heart, a simple thank you, a quiet I love you, the sincerity of a grateful message vibrates around the room for all to feel.

As I listened to the messages of honor given to Mr. Ron Hancock, a man who leads from his heart, serving others without thought of return, I realized that I was in the presence of an individual who lived his life's purpose fully and completely. Believing in young leaders who came to him with grandiose ideas, he found a way to nurture their sense of wonder, encouraging them along the way.

A message beyond words, a connection transcending this moment in time, an invitation to be recognized, acknowledged, valued....a man of service honored by a former student committed to living his life with pure intention, genuine conviction to stay true to his path, inspired to create a larger ripple, a greater impact on this world.

A seeker of knowledge shares admiration with a spirit of light. A spirit of light acknowledges a guide along life's journey. Life's journey weaves among individuals who cross paths for a week, a year or a few years interconnected by one thread, one spirit. A ripple of genuine love continues today with each interaction and each intention for creating heartfelt memories.

❧ Messages within the Chaos

The day began with an invigorating conversation about manifesting what we desire in life and being open to the signs along the way. As David and I walked around Manhattan, we noticed that people hurried, rushed, and appeared preoccupied with the thoughts swirling in their minds. Honks, sirens, busyness, and a sense of rush, rush, rush filled the streets on this midweek work day.

"What is your message?" was contemplated. As we journey through life we sometimes forget the power of a magical moment meeting a stranger, offering gratitude for service in a restaurant and watching the grin widen as the waitress feels the authenticity of an interaction. As we journey, we are bombarded with advertisements on cars, billboards, buildings, signs, and buses. So often, we walk and walk and never notice the message or consider the implication for our life. Instead, journey with intention, focus with possibilities swirling in our being, and stay present to all who cross our path.

We walk and inhale the surroundings around us, messages begin to appear and leave an imprint of significance on our lives. Simple messages, short interactions, common words take on a new meaning in our life today. A large billboard reads *Expect Everything* and in a moment, the full understanding of this message resonates within me. We can "expect everything" we desire or we can expect all the calamities of life. We have a choice at every moment of living. We can breathe in peace or we can inhale the tension that ruminates in the air as commuters rush to work. We can fuse our dreams into our reality by feeling it as truth. The magic lies within our hearts when we experience fulfillment and embrace the possibility of our dreams. Inspiration emerges when we become committed to our dream remembering that we can make a difference in one moment.

Simple messages speak to our spirits. Our souls yearn for peacefulness within the chaos. A sign with the words *Peace Be with You* speaks to us so we cross the street to discover a statue of St. Francis of Assisi inviting the animals to rest upon his body. The simple statue draws us to open a door with the number 333 over its entrance, and we discover a hidden outdoor chapel tucked away between the majestic towering skyscrapers. We notice that the light shines through this small open spot. The mosaics depict individuals who made a difference in their lifetime through simple acts of kindness, through steadfast faith, and through a commitment to their dreams. We light candles delicately placed within the red candle holders. I think of love and the power of one's heart pausing to remember those who have left a heart print on our souls. We enter a chapel to discover a service in process. A few minutes go by and we hear the preacher sharing his powerful message. "You can't do it alone. I am the vine and you are the branches. Connect with God and ask for whatever you want and it will be done for you! It is like love and marriage: that you may become one with the connection to God and bear much in a life filled with blessings and gifts. Vines bear fruit when there is a connection. Be authentic and go rejoicing in life."

Inspiration from within occurs when we allow our light and the flow of energy to emerge. We evolve and recognize the experience of love. We begin to share dreams and desires, each noticing their own signs.

Feeling the stress of many who hurriedly pace their life to get on to somewhere while forgetting to go within to discover the power of one's resilient spirit, reminds me of the gifts that I provide others by empowering them to see beyond their current situation. This gift to discover the power of transforming obstacles into opportunities, and to live life fully creating connections along the way. By going within and finding the stillness, we can bring peace to this world. We can emanate love, joy and peace

EVEN when we are surrounded by the chaos of a metropolitan hustle and bustle. As we journey through this world, we are reminded to love and to remain open to receiving for all that we desire will be presented to us. Ask and it shall be given. A desire to create a joyful experience, a peaceful contemplation among the chatter of a noisy city has been achieved. Being fully present to the laughter of the day, the symbolism of the messages, and the possibility of the dream continue to resonate within me as I am open to the next new day when the universe swirls inside my soul.

↦ Soul Connections

When we share from our soul, we connect beyond time and space.
We feel without expressing words.
We hear a message within one's tone, feeling it in our being.

When are we open and when are we closed?
Do we feel the vulnerability and then pull away?
Do we connect and then disconnect?
Is it worth connecting only to say good bye?
Do we keep separate so we never have to feel?

Limits are only imaginary...
We can create all that we feel and experience.
When we feel safe, we create balance within and balance between others.
It brings us to a higher place, a higher sense of self.

Let it be.

↔ The Light of a New Day

The full moon peers through the plane window radiating light to all who see. The moon shines like the light within our hearts, simply being present high in the sky, radiating light in all directions like the rays of a sun on a sparkling day. As I look upward toward the moon, light emanates in the darkness of the night. The moon's aura radiates hope and possibility for the journey ahead. Stars sprinkled in the sky blend with the lights of the cities below. A union of sky and earth, a blanket of darkness joins together forming one union of heaven and earth. A silence of destiny blankets the earth on this early morning. What one may see as separate during the day now takes on a continuity of spirit, a connection that transcends time and space. All appear as one.

Below on the resting earth, one might mistakenly feel it is void of life, darkness blends together, sprinkled with the scattered lights of small towns, meandering roads and street lights in various directions. Looking outward, I wonder….

In life, sometimes what seems like a dark moment is actually an unfurling of the light within. What may appear as void is actually full of vibration, full of possibility, full of connection, transcending what we know in a moment in time. What we may pass ever so briefly can fill our souls with light and "knowingness" that a simple moment in time can leave an imprint on our lives. Traveling high above the cities below, passing for ever so briefly a moment, yet feeling a sense of connection with the lights below, I consider what is unfolding in this new day.

Lights sprinkled throughout the earth, the simplicity of a moment in time, a fleeting transition between night and day reminds me of the essence of the light within each of us. A simple conversation, a presence within a room, a light shared unconditionally with another can offer rays of strength for those feeling darkness in their life. Living from one's heart spreads rays of love, invisible like the darkness of the night, yet as powerful as this moment in time that I glance out the window, not knowing where I am, yet feeling the vibration of the lives that are preparing to awake for another day on planet earth.

As I look out the window again, the lights strengthen, the patterns seem to suggest a city lies below; a connection of strangers waiting to interact on this new day. As the lights blend to form a pattern, connected, yet separate, I realize that we are all light that when connected from the heart of unconditional love and support, the strength of the bond seems to transcend an experience. The light remains no matter where we travel, inwardly in a moment of meditation, outwardly as we interact with others, silently as we pause with gratitude, vibrantly as we laugh with a friend, compassionately as we serve without being asked. The light remains within our souls when we allow ourselves to let go of our limiting thoughts, release the imagined boundaries, and consider a new possibility. The light remains when strangers share a dream and another says "I believe in you." The light remains when we allow ourselves to be vulnerable to the greatness that lies within ourselves, not knowing the *how* yet trusting the inner light that shines when eyes look sincerely at one another, when silence exchanged during a hug says *I love you* or when the spirit of *being all that I am* radiates throughout a room.

I glance out the window again and I discover a blanket of snow while hours before I was embracing a brilliant sunset in Long Beach. Just as life unfolds each day, the possibilities of the dreams within our hearts begin to unfold, transcend the swirling thoughts that seem to hold us back. How can I do it? Will it work? Can I take the risk? Will others understand? As the night turns to day and darkness turns to light, a fleeting moment reminds me that the simple interactions at the training I just experienced offer a complete and full understanding of the shared responsibility we have on this planet to radiate unconditional love and support, one stranger at a time, one family member at a time, one coworker at a time.

✎ The Ripple Effect

Looking at the meandering creek, I feel the brisk wind against my cheek. The wind rustles the trees and even kisses the leaves transforming the color from green to an early autumn blossom or orange and yellow. While my body craves the warmth of summer, I open to the brisk pace of fall, remembering that life is cyclical just like the seasons. Noticing the glistening sun against the water, I see the ripples within the calm surface. Without noticeable presence, the wind carries the water in a uniform, distinguishable ripple that vibrates across the water until it touches the shoreline.

The ripples seem to grow as I slow down long enough to notice. Their patterns mesmerize the onlooker, capturing the imagination of one's mind. Can a simple moment in a day hold this much beauty? Can the simple action of pausing to contemplate a corner of a creek bring such internal warmth? Can the fallen leaves that swirl within the ripples signify the power of one's interaction with another in life?

This snapshot, this moment in nature, rekindles the spirit of life, the essence of simple moments, and the power of one's choices. In life, we can be the wind that creates the ripples of kindness, and love and joy in the world. We can be the water that carries the positive interactions to others. We can become the shoreline that offers support and a sense of guidance for others. We can be the leaf that may have come from another location yet surrenders to the path that it is on and makes the best of new situations. Collectively, when the wind, water, leaves and shore join together, they form a partnership, an ebb and flow of unity, a connection of spirit. As they meander along, they are unaware of the beauty they have created for a passerby who stops to notice.

In life, our actions, our words, our feelings all are part of a larger ripple. It can come in the form of an interaction of one human to another, one stranger who becomes a friend, one soul who speaks to another soul without even realizing the impact, its power or its legacy. When one person smiles at someone in need, a heart lightens. When one person offers a genuine compliment to a hard working employee their day may become brighter. When one person holds the intention that all people matter, the ripple of unconditional love becomes like the wind—an invisible power that transcends time and space.

When, we as humans, live with love in our hearts, a ripple of kindness spreads, connects one to another, creates a path in the journey of life that allows others to float through life's challenges. We can offer a sense of peace by our existence within this world, by seeing what is possible, by believing that one simple moment in time can inspire and empower others to consider more, to capture more, to be more.

As I inhale the beauty of this moment, this simple meandering creek high in the mountains speaks to me. I realize how it just "is" and yet its message is profound. In our ability to be, to interact with others with joy in our hearts, I believe it is possible to create this same peace that I felt simply by noticing a creek.

⟜ The Stream of Allowing

As I ride along the Stowe Bike Trail, I notice the ripples of water in the river. I glance at the ripples that are formed. As the water brushes against the rock, the flow of the river seems to take a new path, similar, yet varied depending on the rocks in the river. To some, they may appear as obstacles; to others just a guide in the path of the water. In life, it seems that we can allow the rocks in our path to be obstacles or opportunities. We can flow with the changes in life or we can become stuck and buried in the challenge. It often depends on the meaning that we give the situation that determines if we allow life to unfold or if we ruminate over the block that we are experiencing.

Noticing the flow of the river, I feel a sudden drop in temperature. Glancing above, the sun hides beneath a darkened cloud hiding the glow of the sun. For a moment, the resiliency of the day, the glistening water, and the sparkle of the moment seems to hide behind the blackened sky. How often in life do we focus on the darkness instead of the possibilities that lie in the light ahead? How often do we focus on the challenge instead of the lesson hidden within the experience? As quickly as the darkness set in, it floats away and the sparkling sun kisses the ripples of water in the river.

I view the surroundings and notice the blossoming of autumn colors on the trees. Golden leaves wave in the wind. Amber colors flap in a rhythmic pattern. The white and black beauty on the trunk of a birch tree offers a stark contrast against the majestic colors of burgundy, orange and yellow on the adjacent tree. By pausing for a few moments, I realize that I allowed myself to reflect and receive, to consider and to ponder, to create and to be. A few moments in my journey offered me the spirit of being fully present to the messages of nature and fully open to receiving a new message. For me, today, I am open to allowing the flow of a river to remind me to live in the present, surrendering to the changes in the day, continuing with the ebb and flow of creating my dreams and to receive all the insights that pausing for a few moments have given me. I continue on my ride, inhaling the beauty of the earth and sky.

∽ Unconditional Love of Friends

Stars sparkle high in the sky,
I think of friends, near and far,
The power of unconditional love,
Shines like Brilliance Above,

The journey of friendship expands,
Trust grows, honesty beckons, hearts open.

Being in the presence of a true friend allows us to open up to
new insights,
No longer pretending, rather expressing, feeling and connecting…
No words need to be spoken, no conditions of friendship,
No expectations to be anything other than me…

An understanding heart listening without judgment,
A caring presence when life seems overwhelming,
Compassion shared when life brings a challenge…
Someone who simply knows what to say, even before you have shared
your story.

Simple actions, kind gestures, endearing moments…
leave imprints on our hearts, minds, and souls.
A moment in time when someone cared openly,
suspending their own needs for another.

The stars sparkle, the connections transcend time and space.
Memories fill our heart, whispers of days gone by…

✢ Until the Next Rainbow

The dew's aroma of this early morning fills my room as I awake. With windows open, the birds sing a glorious song. Committed to my goal of daily exercise, I roll out of bed for a 5:30 AM walk with a friend. The earth is covered with the kiss of rain and the darkened clouds unfold a stormy day. A text message confirms that my friend is not joining the walk. Instead of feeling disappointment, I change footwear and head into the woods for a run. Amazed at myself for being able to get up early each morning, and celebrating the ability to breathe and run simultaneously, I listen to inspirational songs as I "learn to run." I find myself fully absorbed with the lyrics of the music…*Go the Distance, Reach, Believe*… and am unaware of the effortless distance I am traveling, fully inhaling the glistening sun as it peeks through the rain-drizzled trees. Noticing the opening of this new day, I stay on course, meandering on the path in the forest. Fueling my conviction to complete my books, I run with passion for the messages that can be shared with others. Squirrels scamper, birds frolic from tree to tree and our earth opens to a new day.

Discovering the resilient spirit within, I run faster and faster. I find myself filled with the possibility of all that can be created and even find enjoyment at being able to run for exercise later in life! I am mesmerized by the transient earth that we live on. A few months ago, a barren forest stood quiet in the coolness of an Upstate New York winter and today a canopy of leaves overhang above this path. The water that poured down in the darkness of night evaporates, creating a mystical mist on this early morning. Will the day cover the earth with more rain or will it awake with the sparkling sun?

The wind jostles the trees and the sprinkles cover me. Lost in my thoughts, I consider the possibilities of the completion of this project. I feel the joy and inspiration the stories will bring to others. Self-created due dates pass, yet the conviction of my heart remains. On this June day, I feel the pulse of possibility emerging. I hear the message of this forest as its seasonal transformation reminds me of the resilient spirit that lives within each of us. We can focus on our goals, modify our plans, stay open to the possibility, and trust the messages that emerge on the path we call life. We can look up and remember that we are never alone when we are fully present in this moment.

When we put aside challenges of days long ago, worries of what is to come, we embrace this moment. When we honor our dreams by taking one step each day toward its fulfillment, we create our path. When we allow the ebb and flow of life to touch our vision, yet not deter our vision, we accomplish all we want. When I integrate flexibility into my life, I discover that a simple change in plans on this dew-kissed morning opened me to the possibility that answers lie all around me, that I can endure the challenges of yesterday only to discover the power of this day, this moment....

I carry the wisdom of this forest within me and I commit to completing this book. Upon returning home, I yearn for a moment of silence on this day when the darkness of storms before and the sunshine of the day to come surrounds me. The sun dances behind darkened clouds. I pause before entering my home, looking out to the horizon. I notice a gentle rainbow pouring out of the sky as if spilling the light that hides within the cloud of uncertainty. Pouring from the heavens to touch this earth, in this corner of my world, I am reminded that with every moment, an opportunity to reconnect with my spirit, reconnect with my essence, reconnect with my dreams exists.

And in this moment, I celebrate you for creating time to read this book, to open to the sparkling moments of this day...and until the next rainbow...may you discover the Wisdom in THIS Moment....

✦ Within the Pause

In the moment when a loving comment is shared and a glance connects one soul with another, within this pause, miracles happen.

In the moment when one breathe anchors the awareness that we are all dancing in the energetic flow of divine possibility, hearts open.

In the moment when we free ourselves of what might not work and live in the landscape of faith and trust, we discover that all that emerges is part of the plan.

In the moment when we quiet the chatter of confusion, fear and uncertainty, we connect with the contemplation of peace within our soul.

In the moment when we laugh fully, we breathe in the vibration of wholeness, of joy and of love, a fullness of life that can be captured when we pause and integrate all we experience.

When we pause…we discover that we are all individuals yearning to live life fully, passionately and with vitality that creates health and happiness in all.

When we pause…we hear the whisper of our heart, we discover that the wave of possibility that creates a world where people connect deeply, support unconditionally and transform this planet is very real.

When we pause…we release all that holds us back from our dreams, the limitations and considerations evaporate, opening our souls to the light that emanates from all of us.

When we pause…we connect with *knowingness* that each stranger is a friend, each challenge is an opportunity to reach within and unfurl our greatness, and each idea can be manifested into an event that transforms life as we once knew it.

Pausing…connecting…discovering…contemplating…knowing that one experience can forever change a life. One conversation can inspire another to believe in their dreams. One connection with a stranger can become the catalyst for new business ideas, inspired actions and a journey to an inspired world!

Pausing…considering…viewing…individuals as whole, even though life may present challenges, letting go of what was and allowing the flow of creativity, health, abundance, joy and love into our paths.

Feeling a "knowingness" that by trusting your intuition, the seemingly gentle nudges to forge ahead, you discover that within a pause there are answers, insights, and the contemplation of your soul's work.

Within a pause, strength, courage, faith and inspiration….
a breathe that invites us to inhale and accept who we are, not who others want us to be or think we are, rather a discovery of our fullest potential, our inner magician who knows we can transform any obstacle into an opportunity.

Within a pause, a feeling of being grounded reminding us that we are all connected on this journey in life. In our *beingness* of who we really are, a wave of healing travels on this planet. A visionary contemplating what is possible in our work and within our families, transcending all